T0049474

Praise for

The Tale of a Wall

"*The Tale of a Wall* is the reason we have literature. Nasser has made art out of poison with his honesty and golden pen...It helps us understand the consequences on others when we do not wield whatever power we each hold for solidarity. A profound and important work."

—Sarah Schulman, author of *Let the Record Show*
and *Conflict Is Not Abuse*

"It is rare to come across a book with such astonishing generosity and clarity. *The Tale of a Wall* is beautiful for its ability to examine the harsh realities of oppression with lush prose that creates its own uncompromising terrain. Nasser Abu Srour's story, which he wrote while condemned to a lifetime sentence in an Israeli prison, is further proof that no wall can restrain the imagination, no bullet can kill the idea of freedom."

—Maaza Mengiste, author of *The Shadow King*,
short-listed for the 2020 Booker Prize

"Abu Srour's memoir is more than a tale of prison. His unflinching prose reveals a powerful truth: human beings are compelled to tell our stories in order to affirm our existence in an unjust world. Ultimately, he captures both the individual and collective spirit of Palestinians who, to this day, continue to resist dispossession, disillusionment, and despair."

—Sahar Mustafah, author of *The Beauty of Your Face*

"An extraordinary memoir. Abu Srour is not just a witness of his personal life but a witness to one of the major tragedies of our times."

—Amara Lakhous, author of *Clash of Civilizations Over an Elevator in Piazza Vittorio*

"Here, at a historical moment when Palestinian prisoners are again discussed only as a collective political lever, Nasser Abu Srour writes from Hadarim Prison about love, endurance, loyalty, and freedom. His voice rises above the wall of his desert cell, above his confession-under-torture and thirty years in the Israeli penal system, above his life sentence and Israel's broken promise to release him during the Obama-era peace negotiations. Fierce, lyrical, and defiantly beautiful, his testimony is full of generosity and white-hot courage. He turns his imprisoning wall into an instrument of his soul's freedom. For the reader, that wall becomes a mirror: an instrument of empathy and conscience. You will come away with a heart full of resolve—to work for solidarity, justice, and mercy."

—Sarah Cypher, author of *The Skin and Its Girl*

"In contemplating the meaning of freedom, and the prison walls enclosing him, Nasser Abu Srour has produced a richly emotional and affecting memoir. His poetic prose, lyrically translated by Luke Leafgren, ranges far beyond physical confines to evoke steadfastness and universal human dignity, through the intellectual curiosity of a writer 'born into a family on the margins, living in a marginal place filled with marginal people.' Its resonance, and Abu Srour's vision, are far from marginal."

—Matthew Teller, author of *Nine Quarters of Jerusalem*

"A stunning book. A poetic and remarkable account of decades of imprisonment and the effect it can have on the mind, body, and soul. This is a story of unimaginable loss, but also of survival."

—Sally Hayden, author of *My Fourth Time, We Drowned*

THE TALE
OF A WALL

The
TALE
of a
WALL

REFLECTIONS
ON THE MEANING OF
HOPE AND FREEDOM

NASSER
ABU SROUR

Translated from the Arabic
by Luke Leafgren

OTHER PRESS
NEW YORK

Originally published in 2022 as حكاية جدار by Dar Al Adab, Beirut
Copyright © Nasser Abu Srour, 2022

English translation copyright © Luke Leafgren, 2024

"I do not love you, death" on page 228 by Samih al-Qasim (1939–2014). Translated
by Luke Leafgren.

Production editor: Yvonne E. Cárdenas
Text designer: Patrice Sheridan
This book was set in Arno Pro by Alpha Design & Composition
of Pittsfield, NH

10 9 8 7 6 5 4 3 2 1

All rights reserved. No part of this publication may be reproduced or transmitted in
any form or by any means, electronic or mechanical, including photocopying,
recording, or by any information storage and retrieval system, without written
permission from Other Press LLC, except in the case of brief quotations in reviews
for inclusion in a magazine, newspaper, or broadcast. Printed in the United States of
America on acid-free paper. For information write to Other Press LLC, 267 Fifth
Avenue, 6th Floor, New York, NY 10016. Or visit our Web site: www.otherpress.com

Library of Congress Cataloging-in-Publication Data
Names: Abū Surūr, Nāṣir, 1969- author. | Leafgren, Luke, translator.
Title: The tale of a wall : reflections on the meaning of hope and freedom /
Nasser Abu Srour ; translated from the Arabic by Luke Leafgren.
Other titles: Ḥikāyat jidār. English
Description: New York : Other Press, [2024] | "Originally published in 2022
as حكاية جدار by Dar Al Adab, Beirut."
Identifiers: LCCN 2023040739 (print) | LCCN 2023040740 (ebook) |
ISBN 9781635423877 (paperback) | ISBN 9781635423884 (ebook)
Subjects: LCSH: Abū Surūr, Nāṣir, 1969- | Political prisoners—Palestine—
Biography. | Palestinian Arabs—Biography. | Palestinian Arabs—
Social conditions.
Classification: LCC HV6295.P3 A28 2024 (print) | LCC HV6295.P3 (ebook) |
DDC 365/.45092 B—dc23/eng/20231221
LC record available at https://lccn.loc.gov/2023040739
LC ebook record available at https://lccn.loc.gov/2023040740

To Mazyouna, who no longer sees.

To Nanna, who saw beyond me.

And to Shatha, who sees me.

Thus Spoke the Wall

Dear Reader:

At first glance it may appear that the pages you hold in your hands are the timid offering of an imprisoned man who decided, after long hesitation, to take the plunge and write. But no! This is not my story. I am merely a witness, providing my testimony to the events I have seen and heard. This is the story of a wall that somehow chose me as the witness to what it said and did. The sentences of this text could not have been composed without the support of that single, solid source: the wall. They would have broken apart and scattered to the winds but for the wall's abiding care. Since the beginning of my journey, the wall has given me all my defining traits and all the names I have been known by—in the camp, on the outskirts of the city, in prison, and in the heart of a woman.

I am the voice of this wall. This is how it decided to speak. It is a prison narrative, with all the illness, chaos, and confusion of such a tale. This text is not the child of any late-night discussion in some intellectual café, seated around a table crowded with drinks and stories. No! It was birthed from the womb of a concrete wall, a wall so hard it barely shows the words I etch upon it. It is a text born of iron and concrete.

I wrote using all the words and phrases I possess. Sometimes I separated them, and sometimes I tied them together. As I wrote, I held fast to every word of the wall's dictation, following the rules that apply to it alone. I wrote like someone come to deliver a few final remarks before the clock stops ticking. I wrote without any literary devices, apart from those that the wall insisted upon. I wrote because reading in a time of sterility has become a cowardly act.

And I wish you all a rugged time of reading it!

Nasser Mazyouna Abu Srour

PART ONE

Me, My Lord, and a Most Confining Place

Letting Go and Holding Fast

Two weeks ago, I emerged from an extended bout of apathy and decided to read a book by Kierkegaard. In the book he talks about love, arguing that the best way to preserve it is to release the beloved and to deny all possessive instincts, such as dependency and egotism. He also claimed that this letting go is only possible through the irrationality of faith.

Reading that piece was not easy for me. My prison cell was suddenly filled with the question of "how." The cell had to expand to create room for the flood of questions that surged from the man's argument. That kind of stretching was something my cell did only rarely—and I never knew if it was for my sake or its own. After an hour, the doors were still closed and locked. Yet somehow, being locked up with those questions became an invitation to seek possible answers.

As I see it, everything begins with a question, and certainty is the child of doubt. How is it that we let go, by the power of irrational faith, all that is transitory for the sake of an infinite Supreme Being? How do contentment and acceptance arise from letting go? How does clinging to a wall become the shortest path for crossing through to the other side? Is it truly rational for your own hands to tie your bonds? For your heart to be filled with love directed toward no specific object?

What follows is the reply that came to those questions and to many other wonderings that arose during my long years of detention. This is the answer that came when the instincts for control, domination, and clinging were countered by an act of letting go.

The journey begins by letting go of everything you once believed: you, who have worn a thousand "I"s. Each of them spoke through you, and you believed each of the countless narratives, even as you changed with each "I" that you pulled on. Sometimes you kept the faith, and other times you shook off the religious heritage that weighed you down. A freedom fighter one day, and the next day a slave to a reality that allows you to glimpse heaven's gift, even if its details shatter your existence. You sanctify every object around you, without any holiness left for yourself. One minute you are master of your domain, which you fill with your own words and meanings. The next you are held hostage to an alphabet invented in some other time, for someone else's purposes. Then all your wondering gets buried deep inside you, your questions turn into doubts, your doubt becomes error, and your erring bursts into a flame from which you cannot escape. You are lost in the darkness of past eras that refuse to end. You are enveloped by the gloom of cultures that possess no sun to illuminate their darkness, no moon to give them beauty.

So where do you turn? There's no escape from yourself except into yourself, for you only become you when you let go of your secondary selves and hold fast to your single unique identity. That self steps forward to bestow names and descriptions upon the elements of your existence, suffusing them with meaning. Now you are firmly established within yourself as a self that has been liberated from the religious, social, and political repressions that formerly conferred a sense of protection. Each of those repressions performed violent acts upon you. They drew up charges and forced you to defend yourself until all your defenses faltered and you became the first to condemn yourself.

Once you let go of all of that, it becomes possible for you to reconcile with that which you really are, something you previously thought was a deformed copy of yourself. Now it is possible to arm yourself anew with a mural of yourself, painted with all your selves. You find a place for it within an internal geography containing no contradiction, no strife, no rivalry. None of your selves denies the others or passes judgment upon them. None insists that its voice is now you, all that is within you, all that you say and hold back, all that you communicate, all you are forced to conceal.

As the questions got bigger, so did the apprehension I felt on behalf of my cell. But that didn't stop me. I went back to the winter of 1993, back to cell number 24 in the interrogation block of Hebron Prison and the two words I etched on the wall there: "Farewell, world!" At the time, I knew nothing of Kierkegaard and his letting go. But it seems I've known from the beginning that I had to let go of the possibility of freedom and embrace that wall if I hoped to survive. Without realizing it, I was letting go of freedom as a question that demanded an answer. Yet by doing so, I preserved it as a dream, forever beautiful until the moment it failed to be realized. In this way,

I was like every other Palestinian aware of their bondage, who has to lose their freedom in order to be free, who has to die in order to live.

My flirtation with the wall began early. Throughout all the years of a confinement that kept moving as though life depended upon it, the wall remained my single point of stability. I made it my stable point of reference, by which I calculated the location, speed, and distance of every element around me. And no, I did not become the center of that universe. Instead, I found my place within it. From that stable place, a person is able to grasp the position of the stars, the grains of sugar that go into a morning coffee, the quantity of sunrays that steal through a window looking out to nowhere, or the diaphanous fabric of a beautiful companion's dress when the night falls.

And so, in the moment that I embraced it, my wall abandoned its physicality and safeguarded all the intentions and aspirations I planted within it. It was at a loss, for how could a wall restrict the freedom of someone who has already relinquished his freedom? A person who clings to the wall so hard he almost chokes it, who flirts with it like a lover, and who practices all his usual habits, even his most private ones, under its wing. Someone who recounts incredible deeds that the wall might believe, not knowing any better. Other times, that person explains Kant's noumenon to the wall, arguing that the reality of things is not outside our perception and sensation. If he fails to convince the wall, he scatters the board and sets the pieces anew, for things are what we want them to be.

I thought that when I finished reading Kierkegaard's book, I would escape all the uncertainties and questions that it sparked within me. But suddenly, carelessly, it launched my thoughts on a journey through time, so far I believed there was no coming back. Across luminous distances, I gazed upon the various stages of my life, with all their details, events, and figures, some real and others mere figments of my imagination. I was suspended between the present in which I lived and another time that told a familiar story, in which all the faces resembled my own. In that multidimensional time, I floated weightlessly for days. No sensations reached me, no physical laws imposed their customary definition of things. With a feverish instinct of self-preservation, I resolved to fall, clutching everything that had been hung upon me and everything that I had hung on to for nearly half a century. Mechanically, without thinking, I dropped the account of that plunge upon these pages, as though something there might restore my sense of safety.

I came to see that everything that happened in my life—and is happening still—was part of a grand design to unite me with that wall in that cell.

In the Beginning

None of us chooses his beginning. But through the efforts of our short lives, as we discover our immediate environment and expand the boundaries of that circle, each of us begins to ask questions about when, how, and whither.

The quest for beginnings proceeds from our doorsteps. The prologue to our first deeds can only be written with reference to our surrounding environment and the prevailing moral systems and social structures. Starting with our parents, some of those around us treat us as an object of guardianship, and they exert various types of authority, control, and oppression upon us. As we grow older, the familial and societal authorities multiply, choking our path with rules and signposts. Long lists of cautions, resentments, and affections are imposed upon us, together with conflicting instructions about how to apply them. Every attempt to elude the time-worn shackles of family, society, and tradition is foiled. There is nowhere to hide from a discourse in which the imperative mood is the first, last, and essential form of the verb.

I was born in a refugee camp near a place that is still called the City of Peace, even though all Bethlehem has known of peace is its absence. When the prophet of love departed that city with his gospel of glad tidings, he abandoned the city to a forest of spears. My father knew nothing of this city's history, and had he known, I don't think it would have bothered him all that much. In my father's eyes, the Messiah was like all the other prophets, who said many things he did not understand. Nor, I think, would he have been interested in their words had he understood them. My father had other things to worry about, and the only prophets he recognized were the ones who foretold the need to flee their village two hours before the invaders arrived. Two hours, that is, before he began his own barefoot march, leaving behind in a single day everything he had ever known, and carrying nothing besides a naive faith that heaven was watching over him.

The Messiah's city of Bethlehem was the place that received my father. It had eaten its last supper, and there was nothing left on the table for a young man in his twenties, who until the day before, was accustomed to eating the fruits of his own labor after washing the sun's scorching heat from his brow. That young man did not expend much effort understanding the psychology of the land or analyzing the chaos of seasons and their revolutions. As a boy, he had learned to accept whatever fell from the sky, just like the prophets, and he saw no use in complaining. Within a few months, Bethlehem built him a camp, financed by the joint efforts of kings, sultans, and presidents—figures who, until the previous day, my father believed to be imaginary characters in the rambling stories of my grandfather.

A few years passed as my father moved from one job to another, working for people who spoke a language he didn't understand, and built odd-looking houses. In the end, he was able to save enough money to get engaged. My mother was not yet fourteen when they got married, and she needed my father's help to complete her education in managing a household. Starting with five senses sharpened by the coarseness of camp life, that village girl quickly became mistress of the tent, acquiring all the necessary experience and skills to begin her difficult task.

My father, for his part, performed his manhood expertly, and I was the fifth child who testified to his virility. Between the first Nakba in 1948 and the second in 1967, my father chalked up eight victories. The birthing cry of each tiny replica testified to the survival instinct and a desire to compensate for losses that my father knew could never be recovered. In this way, and with conscious forethought, my father burdened us with requiting everything that had been stolen from him: his past and his present, his land and all the creatures that crawled upon it, his dreams—both the small and the medium ones—and many other things that never even crossed his mind.

At the same time, my father suffered under the pressure to provide for a household whose numbers exceeded his modest abilities and skills, even before the addition of my grandfather and grandmother. The burdens of life would have been too much for him were it not for the sensitive female intuition of my mother, who belonged to a long line of women who perceived the inability and failure of their husbands and went out to join the labor force, ignoring the social disapprobation that their minor rebellion aroused. Thus, on account of new economic factors in the 1980s, our family entered a matriarchal era under the authority of the mother.

My father exercised his authority and sought to direct our lives according to instinctive drives as well as methods inherited from time-honored and still-flourishing social structures. Yet, by applying those laws, customs, and traditions—which were reinforced by the anxiety of the Occupation and its threat to the social fabric—my father became their victim. I observed the consequences of his parenting methods on my older brothers and sisters. But poverty tempered my father's masculinity and his domineering nature, and he submitted to my mother's appropriation of authority that, until just a few months before, had been his by rights. He did not show any resistance to speak of, and the transfer of power occurred peacefully.

After my father lost so much of his control to my mother, he began to uncover new aspects within himself, which benefited my younger siblings and me the most. He became closer to us and he no longer looked at us with fear in his eyes. He acquired a renewed ability to listen and hear; he began to marvel at the things he saw. I was the luckiest of all my siblings. After spending many long evenings close by his side, I became his favorite, something my oldest brother never failed to bring up whenever our father was mentioned.

My father wore his new roles with the expertise of someone deprived of other options. Fully conscious of the reversal of roles, he continued to watch my mother as she embarked upon her pedagogic and economic initiatives. Meanwhile, my mother noticed the looks he cast her way. Socioeconomic transformations had suddenly made her the person in charge, the one to whom all questions were addressed. Without any special knowledge or training, and guided only by a mother's intuition and the consciousness of her weighty responsibilities, my mother quickly developed the ability to make shrewd decisions and employ money for a variety of goals and needs. Contradicting Marx's dictum that freedom is merely a concern of the bourgeoisie, my mother set about expanding the reach of her freedom to new domains, confident that her little ones would be able to put the space she provided them to the best of uses.

For a second time, I was fated to become the prime beneficiary of the atmosphere of freedom that came to prevail in our small house. That time coincided with the beginning of my adolescence, with all its youthful rebellion. I set about exploiting every opportunity to break familial and social strictures. New possibilities for youthful escapades were not the only thing my mother provided to a boy whose appetites exceeded the restrictions of camp life. She also expanded and diversified the food on our table, which in turn developed our sense of taste. Our vocabulary for food was gradually enriched with words to describe the new types of fruit that diversely filled the basket propped in the kitchen corner, a basket that almost sang under the inspiration of the intense colors and smells that passed through it. Meat graced our table one additional day each week, no longer being limited to a single dish of maqluba on Fridays.

My father continued his small job as a used-clothes vendor, selling items that had already known three or more owners before they came into his possession. Every Saturday, he would wake me early in the morning to help him pile his metal cart high with clothes. My task was to deliver the cart to the city market after my father went on ahead to claim a place to exhibit his goods. He could never comprehend why I arrived late each time, and he gave up asking me the reason. How could I explain the two streets that led to the market? One was the short way, and taking that direct route afforded my father many anxious minutes of waiting for a boy weighed down by all the dreams of escape heaped upon his cart. The other road was long, but it skirted far around my school, which reduced the risk of running into my classmates. That usually saved me from futile attempts to hide the tears of shame that wet my face every time I ran into one of my friends—or several of them, if I was particularly unlucky. I don't know what embarrassed me more: my father's cart, filled with false promises, or my father himself, whose impotent hands lacked the means to fulfill them.

The Camp

Surrounding the camp are structures that would have resembled a city had they invested the slightest effort to organize the various parts and erase their internal contradictions. Each building tells the history of the city in its own way. One modern building from the 1970s, for instance, jumps out to grab the attention of passersby and be the first to tell an ancient story about the Holy City. A spotlight is trained upon religious symbols carved into the stone, together with a surreal, pagan-looking image. There's nothing wrong about plucking out just one of the many eras the city has lived through, and depicting the first martyr and savior of the city, with nails to make his hands and feet bleed while he remains hanging there, praying for deliverance.

Across the street is a building from the 1950s whose stones are bare of any symbols. It hides the gods it worships and the names of its prophets, as though recalling the dawn of Islam, when any declaration of faith would call down the wrath of the polytheistic Quraysh tribe. At least, that's what you think until you come closer to the building and discover an engraving that expresses gratitude to the One God, beside whom no second or third can be worshipped.

You believe you have successfully unraveled the successive identities of the city with the eloquence of a PhD student, but then it strikes you with a third element, and the confusion you felt upon entering the city comes rushing back. For the next house—or something that looks like a house—calls out to pilgrims returning from their visit to Jerusalem. It invites them inside to seek a blessing by kissing a stone that has survived for thousands of years after Rachel, wife of Prophet Jacob, reclined there to rest during her journey to Hebron.

Just when this city settles down to harmonize its breathing to the ringing of bells, the calls to prayer, and hymns being sung, my father turns up, along with a whole caravan of people like him who possess no houses at all. So they erect a tent as their cramped home. Before long, that first tent has become a camp. Located in the very heart of the city, the camp nevertheless exists on the margins, feeling indebted for whatever space to live can be found in those margins.

The camp passes through successive stages, beginning with the age of cloth. When the wind blows, it shows no mercy on these little people who have not yet discovered how to root themselves in one place, and they are scattered in every direction. Then comes the age of bricks, an era of international charity that hides their nakedness and weakness, as well as the collusion of those among them who have realized that no imminent return will set them free, and that habituation will make the situation permanent. In the end comes the age of concrete, built by the cheap labor of hands that have decided—after losing their own land—to be rescued by the people who have displaced them. So upon the ruins of their own houses, they labor for the invaders, people who came to find a homeland, believing a promise made to them by their Lord.

I arrived on the scene during the era of weakness and collusion, born into a family on the margins, living in a marginal place filled with marginal people. Like any marginal child, I began exploring my marginal boundaries. I wandered about slowly, feeling no sense of haste. Each hour felt as long as a lifetime, and the number of houses in our immediate vicinity did not exceed the toes on one of my feet—a rough, unshod foot at that. But my feet soon grew stronger and began conveying me with ease through the alleys and cramped neighborhoods of the camp. My body felt more constrained with each passing year. It did not understand the camp's inability to make room for the children growing up there.

Those children had limbs that grew stronger and feet that became impatient of constantly following the same paths. They were curious about the nature and form of all that happened elsewhere, everything outside the neighborhoods that kept shrinking until they stifled our very last breath. Everything elsewhere seemed bigger—the sun, the clouds, the stars. Over there, outside the camp, the people looked so nice. They wore new clothes so often that, seeing them from afar, I imagined that a holiday had paid a visit to their homes and decided never to leave. Who could blame that visitor? The houses over there had pretty white walls, with balconies overlooking small gardens in the back and open plazas in front. I could nearly smell how clean they were. When a holiday visited us, however, I understood why it departed so quickly in the morning: its gifts were so basic, and the disappointments it left behind so heavy, no matter how many dreams children tucked into their pillows before falling asleep.

My adolescent self could not bear standing at the borders of the camp for long. I couldn't keep myself from jumping across and coming close to listen to the legends told by the houses on the outside. I was certain their stories would be better than the boring ones my mother told, with details I couldn't keep straight and happy endings that no longer guaranteed me a good night's sleep. So I jumped. The first thing that caught my eye was the orderly lines of the houses. Their backs were turned to the camp, and I didn't know if that had been done unconsciously or for reasons beyond my understanding. Yet the attitude of those orderly lines suggested a hostile act. The undertone of hostility was subsequently reinforced by the stares of the people there, who had welcomed the holiday into their homes and closed their balcony doors. It was like something from a crime movie, where the young man slips in, impelled by his curiosity, and flits from shadow to shadow until he finds his way back to the camp.

My first encounter with the other side did not inspire any of the terror that would prevent me from repeating the experiment. Indeed, it only increased my curiosity. The road now appeared closer, and everything about it enticed my feet to make another attempt. But this time, I was greatly surprised to find the houses had thrown open their doors. The streets were packed with people celebrating the holiday. Nothing from my first visit had prepared me for this new scene. There was no wall to conceal my tension and my errant footsteps, nothing to hide me from the glares that followed me so intently or the suspicions I was unable to allay. What did that place on the

other side of the wall fear from a boy afflicted by an inordi-
nate degree of God-given curiosity? Or from a mother who
indulged his imagination? From a youth who came before its
time? Or a camp that was strangling its inhabitants?

That imitation city surrounded the camp on all four sides
and locked the gates to prevent any escape. As our houses and
neighborhoods clamored with new souls, the camp looked for
some open space to put them until it gave up and crammed
them in however it could. These children began to inherit
the camp's marginal ways, for nothing the camp said or did
made any difference in the history or geography of a city that
had washed its hands of the camp's story, denouncing as lies
any mention of exile or forced relocation. The city showered
the camp with accusations and minimized its suffering. It
stripped away the camp's diverse identities and resorted to the
dictionary to find every possible synonym for traitor, fugitive,
emigrant, refugee, stranger, exile, alien.

Such words had the effect of dragging the camp away
from the reality of what was, or was not, actually happening. They forced it into a parallel time and place where the
camp began weaving, slowly and methodically, the threads
of its own estrangement. Events were arranged according to
a novel alphabet and told the history of its alienation during
the Nakba. Prior eras were forgotten entirely: the pre-Islamic
era that justified the use of tents, the emigrating prophet who
became lord and master of Medina, the Crusaders and Sala-
din. The history of the camp was devoid of legends. We had no
heroes who rode the clouds, hammer in hand, no generation
peopled by gods, no mortal man who spoke with his Lord, no

sage who walked on water, no prophet who drew water from a stone.

Confined within a narrow, four-sided space and shackled by an alphabet squeezed into letter blocks, the camp had to compose its legend with new symbols, heroes, and events—some of them true and some imagined. Alternate realities. The people were forced to invent the tools and instruments for writing, in case they and their memories grew old, and their vision faltered when organizing the elements of the legend. There was no elite who would write their legend. No one to revive a discourse that would rebuild ruined houses or unlock the doors of any still standing. No one to weave a vision that reunited what had been scattered by the pains of the road and the magnitude of the loss.

As a result, the camp found itself alone and cut off. It was besieged by a different story, one that treated it with disdain, omitted it from all its texts, and never mentioned the destruction of its patrimony. A story that erected high walls between them, too high to climb over, to ensure the purity of its race. So the camp turned toward the children growing up there, children who no longer accepted the camp as their identity, nor felt they belonged there. Those children rejected the camp's borders as the limits of their imagination and repudiated the policies of marginalization.

The second generation of the Nakba waited twenty years to drop from their shoulders the legacy of shackling defeats that were not their own. In 1987, its members announced their revolution and used stones to compose the first pages of their legend. Breasts were bared, arms extended, idols smashed, and glass ceilings shattered. Fathers retreated while sons stepped forward to write their own story. Camp, village, and imitation city...waiting, victory, liberation, return...great dreams and young heroes...a camp, a coast, and a mountain of fire: all elements of an epic that had come true, a legend written upon a wall. A generation that only a day before was hanging from the barriers of its camp, full of doubt, now became master of the place and author of the story. Eyes that used to watch over them now began to regard them with respect. Abandoning its former festivals, the camp celebrated this generation instead. Houses decorated their walls with images of those killed the day before and those who would record the most incredible victory on the morrow. The legend renewed the story of the land. It restored a sense of space and time. It built bridges and tore down walls. It traded the masks of flight and survival for a cloth to wrap around one's face when going out to the fight. It put away pretty words and offered deeds instead. It transformed their fathers' prophetic speeches into broken bones and warm bodies laid in graves.

At the dawn of Islam, a famous covenant was pledged under a sidra tree. But our camp was not able to make any treaty whatsoever with any entity surrounding it, under any available tree, upon any land that embraced or rejected it. Were it not for the legend, the people could never have reconciled with a past that was now buried deep under a land that had once been their own. When a new generation took the place of the former elite, it took the ethos of return and shaped a collective imagination around it, charting the path and minimizing any obstacles or impediments. Their imagination made dreams seem possible once again. Through that legend, the camp recovered an alphabet that had vanished. And now that they've gotten it back, they haven't stopped writing their history in letters that reach to the sky.

Every story has three elements—time, place, and characters—as well as some question that ties the three together. But the camp possessed no time or place to form the necessary elements of its narrative. Long decades of occupation had severed the connection between time and place, which floated off in opposite directions. For those forced to leave their homes, either in the first Nakba or the second, the hands of time had frozen in place. They hung their watches like keys above the tent door in case heaven might send a second Passover at nightfall, a second Exodus to free them from their wretched wandering in the wilderness of exile. Now that the sense of time was lost, events could only be defined as pre-Nakba or post-Nakba. Everything they sowed, half of what they reaped, anything they left in the ground, and whatever the birds ate—all that was pre-Nakba. Everything they were unable to plant, whatever they were incapable of reaping, and all that they denied the birds—that was the post-Nakba era. When place ceases to move through time, it watches young souls carrying grandmothers on their shoulders, together with everything they can load upon their backs, and it fears a universal explosion that scatters the dust without any possibility for a resurrection.

Jacques Derrida said, "There is nothing outside the text." The story of the camp is a text without a time or a place, which makes the camp exist beyond time and place. It writes its own unique story, expending as many sons and daughters as possible for the sake of a breakthrough, whether it comes sooner or comes later. All elements of the story are centered upon that breakthrough. From the first moment the camp began writing its story, I knew a text was waiting for me. At times, I would write that text, while at other times it would write me. Yet I did nothing that was likely to save me, or to ensure a future life that resembled the truncated story being lived by those around me. No! I did just the opposite.

The Intifada of the Stones, 1987–1993

In the fall of 1987, I was about to turn eighteen. I had organized my priorities and felt I was on the right track. My dreams would not be constrained by those long periods of standing at the limits of my camp, churning with jealousy and anger because of what I saw on the other side. A cosmic matrix of suns, moons, and hidden galaxies was helping me to achieve my goals, some modest and others exceedingly complex. Nothing seemed too difficult for the Lord to whom my mother prayed for help in all her ways, casting upon His shoulders her heavy cares and the challenge of meeting the family's expanding needs.

The innumerable stars and celestial bodies in the sky above proved how easy the task could be. As a child, I came to know their movements and their shifting positions, which were all so lovely to me. If I ever felt discouraged, I would simply close my eyes and deprive the heavens of every satellite that lit up its darkness. I knew my mother's Lord could effortlessly accomplish everything in just the same way. All He had to do was exercise His compassion and employ all the letters of the alphabet for my benefit. After all, everything was possible for Him through the divine command: "Be."

God was like the camp: a site of surrender and acceptance, an abridged alphabet, an existence outside time and place. I voluntarily served the Lord who needed only two letters to call everything into existence. The camp, however, held me in its thrall no matter how I answered the question to be or not to be. Divine care continued to manage my affairs, sometimes smoothing out a thorny path and sometimes hindering tasks I was certain would be easy. Having learned every insight I could from two parents whose strong suits did not include negotiation, I spent long hours during even longer nights bargaining with heaven. With all the cunning of one whose senses had been sharpened against the hard borders of the camp, I endeavored to persuade God to improve our conditions, or at least to adjust the terms of the deal.

I kept living my life, and it was as though no time or place existed beyond me. I did not perceive the shadow of other people trying, for their own part, to win the divine care that I had claimed for myself. Others prayed, fasted, and extolled all the holy names. They clung to the faith of obedience and devotion. They got up at the beginning, middle, and end of the night to supplement the five daily prayers with one or two more, as though to win divine approval through sheer force of numbers. Meanwhile, from my place at the border, I was content with pious words expressing trust in a merciful Lord who would save me if I succumbed—or did so repeatedly—to the pull of certain desires.

Certain of my priorities, I began pursuing them with every ounce of strength and energy I possessed. School certificates testified to my efforts and satisfied my vanity. For a time, everything seemed possible. The stars and planets aligned just as I wanted them, so close they brushed my fingertips. It was a clear sign that heaven approved of the plans I was forming for a future beyond the camp, its boundaries, and the people whose presence I took for granted. But that moment was very brief, for the camp, its boundaries, and those people took a different view of things. They possessed a divine care that cared more deeply; the elements of their cosmic matrix were better organized. The crime of snatching a desperate mouthful of bread bound those elements together into a unified society that exploded in rage and rose together in the Intifada of the Stones.

In the intifada, the camp saw a historic moment, pregnant with opportunities. If only the crisis could be managed well, all the doors that had been slammed in the camp's face would open once again. The intifada became the hero of the folktale, except that the legend written by this new hero would supersede all others. The mythological heroes of the past would quit the stage, together with their stories that accepted diverse interpretations.

Very quickly, as though anxious about losing the chance, the camp constructed its stage. Incapable of enduring any more disappointments, it selected its roles, its heroes, and its dialogue like a seasoned professional. Displaced people took the stage, front and center, clothed in bodies that had cast off all the marginal instincts that previously defined them. Soon, in the very first scene of the play, the squares and alleyways were filled with heroes whose blood ran freely when the bullets pierced bodies during their first hurried appearance upon the stage. Nothing about these scenes reminded you of the heroes of Sparta or the defenders of Athens. We had no demigods so tired of the monotony of heaven that they descended to seek immortality through death. The temporality of pain, the spatial locality of suffering, and the finality of death dominated every scene of every act.

The walls of the theater closed in, with pictures and posters displaying elements of the legend. Young souls painted murals of a country, a revolution, and a triangular logo. They rejected a history of quarter-victories or half-defeats. They rejected the limitations of divine promises and prior judgments. These souls turned their backs on speeches that were born and grew up in a land that was no homeland. They turned their backs on the illusion of a community held together by a religion that died in the very moment it set them apart. Instead, these souls fashioned a new imagination. They united a divided people around a homeland—an idea that recalled the physicality of the body and the tangible geography of the land.

Constrained though it was, the theater contained more than enough space for all those taking part in the drama, with room to improvise and exchange roles, characters, and orations. The camp's defining characteristic evolved from separation into union. Isolation became integration. In a remarkable, Darwinian fashion, as though searching for a mate in order to avert the evil of extinction, the walls continued to change color with painted logos and posters, adapting according to successive variations in material and spiritual conditions. By recording the memory of the place, the walls themselves became a principal actor upon the stage of events.

The ability of the elite to lie and the people's need to believe form the two essential elements in constructing any legend designed to establish the laws that subject a society to the power and legitimacy of some regime. Hammurabi of Babylon and the myth of the good king sent by Utu to provide divine guidance to the people; Nüwa, the Chinese goddess who created the ruling elite out of yellow mud and the common people out of brown mud; Purusha, the first human, according to the Hindus, from whose mouth the upper castes were created, while the lower came from his feet: all were legends upon whose lies human societies were unified through laws, rituals, and social norms. Ancient civilizations arose, filling the world with flourishing and decay, death and revival. All that God's prophets needed to do was discredit the lies that had come before.

We needed a generation skilled in shaping new lies into a legend that would repudiate everything we previously believed: the Nakbas, the expulsions, the murders, the futile efforts, the value of submission, the counsel of fathers, the fear of mothers. We needed new lies to believe, and on the altar of their truth we would burn all the offerings we still possessed.

We needed an entire generation of prophets, good at writing upon the walls, good at living through their hearts and their throats. Prophets who would die when crucified and be buried nearby so we could proclaim their lies to the people. Prophets who would dig their own graves and pray one last prayer for our souls when the earth at last became too much for them.

We needed prophets who were members of our own body. Who ate what we ate, built houses that were swept away in the same flood as our own, drank their coffee bitter like us. Prophets who did not get married—or if they did get married, then just to one wife—and if they were unfaithful, would not deny their betrayal or be jealous of their wives like the last males of the tribe had done.

We needed prophets who would turn our suffering into poems of a single line, who would turn our questions into research projects, who would turn our grandmother's stories into alienation, and our exodus into a return. Prophets who would speak a language we understood and turn each of its letters into a cause.

We needed an intifada generation, an autumn generation, one that would drop all the fig leaves covering our nakedness and expose our shame to the shattered mirrors inside us. A generation that would grant us the best title we had ever borne: the Generation of Stones.

Questions

Tell me what you'll fight for, and I'll tell you who you are!

What is it that disturbs your sleep? What dreams startle you awake in the morning? What brings a tear to your eye? Are you anxious when the rains come late? How do you make love? (Or do you prefer a more explicit form of the question?) Upon whose breast do you lay your head when your mother has unexpectedly passed? Does talking to the mirror annoy you? Do you jump when you see your own shadow?

Which prophets do you believe? Does God have a place in your cramped little world? What if it were larger? Are you good at any particular dance? Which defines your poverty: the things you possess, or the things you don't? How do you drink your coffee? If I gave you a choice among all possible things, would you even be able to choose? Are you a Scorpio? Have you ever greeted a woman you didn't know? What kind of woman takes your breath away and stops your heart in its tracks? What does the month of October mean to you? On which side will you be lying when you die? If you were reincarnated, would it still be you, and where would you end up?

Tell me what you'll fight for, and I'll tell you who you are.

These and many other difficult questions weighed upon a youth who had not yet finished his eighteenth year. What is it about such questions that makes a person articulate rebellious answers in a world dominated by tear gas canisters and more important matters? Why didn't I flee the questions when I had the chance? After all, turning and running is the doctrine of survival when bullets fly in a narrow alley. Yet I did not run. I let the questions batter me from every side until each one became an incentive to seek, investigate, and experiment.

Without any attempt to arrange the questions in order of importance, I began my search. The questions were beautiful—that was the first thing I discovered. Beautiful, too, were the possibilities they implied, their promise of arrival, either direct or by some roundabout way. Oh, the magnificence of the questions! And oh, how paltry the answers seemed by comparison! That feeling stuck with me, despite the general sense of postponement that the intifada imposed on so many of my wonderings.

I marveled at how easily my peers found their answers. If the to-and-fro of battle wore them out, they slept upon whatever hard pillow the earth provided them, after having eaten everything that was left on the table—a table they came back to so late that those waiting for them had given up in despair. They slept beside dream lovers who sent them back out in the morning to pursue their dreams. They slept with the intense belief that the revolution would be victorious, even if their belief killed them. I envied that remarkable ability to let go of the questions and hold fast to the comfort of an answer. I envied their exhausted sleep. But I never let go. I met the stubborn questions with an even greater stubbornness, even though it meant my anxiety never relaxed, and I bruised both my right side and my left with all my tossing and turning at night. I never saw a mountain: I saw all that lay beyond it, calling me to discover.

For those taking part, something in the air of the intifada inspired a feeling of the final time: that each thing you did might be the very last. Nothing guaranteed your tomorrow, even when your day was drawing to a close. Kisses you postponed until the following week might grace someone else's mouth, not your own. Deciding not to reconcile with your father after a stupid argument might deprive you of the prayer that would save your soul. An erotic nighttime escapade in which the girl draws back at the last moment might be your most painful loss. A bullet that missed you yesterday might kill you in one hour. The victory flag that you hid under your mother's bed might become your burial shroud.

That meant the time for waiting was over. So, too, was your time for taking things slowly and hoping for a better tomorrow. My time for standing upon the wall was past. Yet all the same, I was unable to abandon that enormous pile of questions, an even larger pile of possibilities, and a hunger that nearly consumed me.

I began to search. And I leave it to your imagination to picture what six years of searching did to an insatiable hunger, to questions that were not satisfied with a single possible answer...

Have you finished imagining that?

I myself have not yet even begun.

Small Gods

The cares, interests, and concerns we choose to focus on say much about us. We grow larger as the interests within us expand, just as we grow smaller when they contract. Every interest that makes its home within us shapes us by determining the contours of our activities, our sleeping hours, what we celebrate around the breakfast table, the songs we listen to, the number of minutes we spend interceding with God, and the titles and prices of the books we buy. The things we defend and the things we love: those are what define us. They are the first things that we declare in the first sentence of introduction, during the first meeting with the first person who asks.

Alongside their own concerns, the Generation of Stones chose to concentrate on other causes: occupied Arab lands whose rulers shrank from the idea of fighting to reclaim them; Arabs who kept quiet while homegrown thieves enshrined their defeats; nationalistic speeches written in foreign languages; billions of poor people surrounded by the hoarded wealth of the world; millions dying of hunger and reduced to numbers, statistics, and averages tucked into the back pages of newspapers in the important and influential capitals; child laborers and their godless taskmasters; cheap labor and even cheaper working conditions; women whose bodies are harassed by violating hands; a women's movement that never gives up the fight; speeches to awaken a paralyzed masculinity…Between one demonstration and the next, between a martyr's funeral and the burial ceremony, Palestinians still found time and emotion to weep over the grief of others. Upon our narrow walls, we made space to write the details of others' suffering until the images and slogans mixed together and became a strange shrine to the existential dignity of suffering. The stones provided by that dignity contained enough hope to compensate for the extra measure of frustration and despair we embraced.

We spoke all the languages of pain. After rejecting prejudice regarding religion, color, or beliefs, our speeches expanded to embrace the entire planet Earth. Our naked, bleeding breasts exposed the lie about a barbarous East that needed the West to refine its primitive savagery. In our lexicon of dignity and worth, the pains of others had no color or smell that distinguished them from our own, for we identified with every speech that rebelled against injustice or supported the not yet triumphant.

Loudly, we rejected tedious panegyrics for kings and sultans. Instead, we read the works of Nâzım Hikmet and Amal Donqol; we read about Võ Nguyên Giáp and Che Guevara. We danced around the fire with the remaining Native Americans. We recited the Fatiha over the souls of a million Algerian martyrs. We ran to cut the noose from around Omar al-Mukhtar's neck in Libya. We filled our arms with as many Arabic books as we could save from destruction by the descendants of Atatürk. We repeated with de Gaulle after his

victory: *Paris is burned, Paris is destroyed, but Paris is liberated.*
We spoke all the languages of pain, but we still had space to
smile and laugh at jokes. We preserved a belief in our coming
victory and a better life, when our long death would die and
we would bury it in the back garden, reciting the poems of
victory we had written for the occasion.

Our public squares ran out of room after embracing all
those cares, but they still existed. In the cramped space that
remained, we played childhood games. We remembered their
loss and our need for an innocence that included mistakes
alongside the certainty of forgiveness, as well as our need
for romanticism, with all its exaggerations. All our women
became the beautiful poet al-Khansa, and all our dead went
to an assured paradise. We praised our poets, even if they
composed just one poem before they died. We recounted
their exploits, some details of which were invented, but who
rebukes a child for lying when he's telling a story? We were
just exaggerating a little!

What are legends if not dreams that frame a long and ardu-
ous task? The romanticism of the rebel taught us to be understanding. Whenever someone wavered or held back, we forgave
them. We created excuses for everyone, even those who could
never find one for themselves. We believed what we read in the
literature of our struggle: that those who do not act commit no
fault. And so we were able to forgive ourselves for all the faults
we committed. We were close to the people, close to their pains
and the hardships of their days. Standing close to their beating
hearts, we sped the pace of our actions as much as they could
bear, and slowed down whenever they became exhausted. The
people believed in our intentions; they believed in us. They

flung open their doors to shelter us. We sought refuge with them and protected them in turn.

The intifada gave causes to us all. It made us small gods. We shaped it in our image and gave it our romanticism, our tolerance, and our forgiveness of transgressions, both small and large. We brought it within the vast space of our cares until it joined the very front ranks. It fought, it resisted, and it spun the small miracles that we desperately needed. Causes are like dreams: they are only achieved when we outgrow them in our understanding, our perception, and our faith in our ability to achieve them. Believing in the universality of oppression and the globalization of poverty was all it took to break free of our provincialisms.

We were not yet twenty years old, yet we devoted ourselves to causes that by now had entered their third millennium. We warred against illusions that debased the human self. We shone a light upon legendary heroes who became gods when they fought and died for their causes. We, too, were gods who bled and died. We were gods without a throne, no heaven to call home, and nothing that we had created out of the void. We decreed nothing, sought no worship, and accepted no one's burnt offerings. We fought with our entire being, we slept when we were able, and we told lies until we were too tired to lie anymore.

We were bigger than our country: our sea, our land, and our sky.

We were holier than our holy places: our mosques, our churches, and our shrines.

We were more delicious than our gardens: our apples, our date palms, and our grapevines.

We were older than our history: Canaan, Adnan, and the Arabic tongue.

We were more eloquent than our poets: Tarafa, Kuthayyir, and King Imru' al-Qays.

We were, we were, we were...

We were lying gods, but we believed our own lies. We believed that Palestine was still possible, that the road was long, and we might not see it in our lifetimes. We believed that freedom was possible, despite all its demands, and that our sacrifices might not be enough. We didn't stop believing for a single day. We would have died, had we stopped believing. We didn't stop fighting for a single day. Without the fight, we would have vanished into thin air. We did not abandon our cause for a single day. Doing so would have made us merely human.

The Arab capitals grew sick from the evils they suffered, and from fervent speeches preaching submission to the reality on the ground. The Arab capitals got so sick they began vomiting up their Palestinian refugees, all those foreign bodies that had wormed their way inside and disturbed their colonial borders. Hoping to be cured of their illness, the Arabs went to the Madrid Conference of 1991, while Palestinians hid themselves away in Oslo and other European capitals to begin bringing an end to the most beautiful of all the lies we had believed.

Unaware of the realities that were being manufactured against our lies, I kept up my lying and my believing until the winter of 1993.

That winter began with my arrest. A life sentence came in its middle. Its end has not yet begun.

A Morning Deferred

January 1993. I spent a cold night at a friend's house outside the camp. I waited for sleep to arrive with the yearning of one exhausted after winning a glorious victory. The morning was approaching fast, as though eager to see how the world appears through the eyes of victors. Where does their sun rise? Upon which side do they pass the night? How does their morning coffee taste, with just a little sugar? After such a triumph, do victors get hungry for breakfast? Do they wash their faces, or will their brow remain smudged with the dust of their victory? I wanted to know what I would look like when I arrived at the university. Would I appear taller? More attractive? Would the girl I liked perceive the signs of my victory and stop ignoring me, as she had been doing in recent months?

I kept loading that morning with expectations and questions until I feared it might never arrive, lest I pile even more burdens upon its shoulders. My two friends had fallen asleep quickly, but the victor's anxiety for his victory drove the sleep from my eyes. So did the ghostly feeling of "the very last time." In that intoxicated, victorious state of mind, nothing guaranteed that morning would arrive, and a single hour could steal from me everything I had achieved that day. Just as a single hour might cart off to hell all memories of my 2:00 p.m. lecture and a conversation with Natalie, the young teaching assistant with revealing attire whom I impressed with my invented descriptions of the knights of the Round Table. Two months earlier, Natalie had invited my friend and me to have ice cream at her house in one of the old neighborhoods of Jerusalem. I think she must have noticed the creative lengths to which this talkative rogue of a refugee went to attract her attention. Such good ice cream! Racing from one memory to another, I slipped below the waves of my exhaustion and slept.

Morning arrived abruptly, hours ahead of schedule. Morning arrived on the barrel of a rifle that smashed against my forehead and shattered delectable visions of Natalie's warm body. The experience did not resemble the common description of death, when a person sees their entire life spooling out before their eyes in a matter of seconds. Instead, the cold steel froze everything. It froze time and place. It froze me, and it froze the man holding the rifle, together with all his reasons and motives. It froze my fear of him and my hatred of everything he represented. The entire frozen universe proceeded toward some undefined intermediate region, where we lost our defining features, our senses, and the demarcation of our roles.

And because the mercy of iron is straight and narrow, the moment ended quickly. Suddenly, we all perceived our roles once again. I was the frightened person whose forehead broke out in a cold sweat from contact with the iron barrel. Facing me was the man with the iron, in all his military dignity. Other men of iron formed a cordon around that time and place. Off to the side were my two friends, deemed extraneous and trying to interpret the scene without the benefit of know-ing the script. There were animals too, barking and straining at the leash, eager to devour every hostile scent in the house if they were only set loose.

Like bursts from an automatic weapon, a strange voice barked a stream of questions at me. A voice with a thick accent that garbled our everyday words. No, this was not death. If I were dead, the voice would be asking about my Lord and my faith, about a prophet coming at the end of the world, and other such things, and I wouldn't have known any of the answers. Instead, these questions were about people and places that I knew very well. All the same, I was incapable of offering any reply. Not out of any refusal or arrogance, but from an inability to speak. Among all the other things that froze, the iron froze my tongue. The questions never ceased, yet I kept failing to pro-duce a sound. Had that voice heard my nighttime plans and the adventures I was dreaming up for the morning? Had it heard about Natalie and her dishes of ice cream, or how the girl I liked was ignoring me? Had it come to spoil my long-awaited entry into the university, confident and triumphant?

Everything paused. Now I was in the center of the scene, on my feet and fully dressed. There were more rifles and out-stretched arms. That was the last thing I saw before being led away to a vehicle reeking of iron and gunpowder, and ringing with the barking of still-ravenous dogs. The voice resumed, repeating questions about yesterday. When did you wake up? Who was beside you? Did you eat breakfast? How much did you eat? Who prepared the food? When did you leave your house? Where did you go? What clothes did you wear? What color were they? Why did you take so long to get ready?

This time, I began answering the questions. My senses were restored by the blows that accompanied them, applied to every inch of my body. It was as though the scene became reality by virtue of the violence that was absent at the beginning. Such a scene could not ring true unless its violent nature were written in as a primary and fundamental element. Nevertheless, between one question and the next, I was amazed at my ability to recall all kinds of images, situations, and conversations. I imagined my parents and their reaction to the news of my arrest. I remembered my last conversation with my sister Inshirah. I could see the girl who ignored me, and I hoped she would cry upon hearing the news. I recalled the taste of the ice cream and the clothes Natalie wasn't wearing that day. Then another question, another photograph to examine, and more stammering answers. Meanwhile, the audible panting of the dogs, coming from somewhere very close, confused my mind more and more.

The vehicle stopped suddenly. Then it drove on, but only for half a minute. It stopped again, and the interior exploded with noisy commotion. Everything inside the vehicle, including the dogs, seemed to crash into me all at once as they exited the vehicle. That was followed by silence for a minute or more. Then, without warning, hands were reaching for my bound hands and feet and I was roughly picked up and half dragged some few meters before they threw me inside some room and slammed the door.

It is difficult to use formal language to describe the interrogation block. The person inside is cut off from their five senses as they knew them prior to entering. A chaos of sensory information detaches them from time, place, and the nature of the objects around them. The words they have accumulated over a lifetime no longer apply, and those who pass through the interrogation block often resort to terms beyond the dictionary when describing their experiences. You see them stumbling over the details, using descriptions with no connection to their objects. The wall is no longer a mass of concrete. Iron chains bend and flex according to the shape of the limbs they bind. The screams of the chained rise to mystical planes. Souls detach from bodies, and the two live completely different experiences.

During the interrogation, time has no meaning. You cease calculating it, no matter how long or short each round of questioning. Place is restricted to the single wall from which they hang you when the questions end. Your needs contract to the only two things that might guarantee your survival: eating in desperate circumstances that have spoiled any appetite, and then banging on the door in case your jailer might materialize, if only for an instant, and grant you the opportunity to void from your body the decaying food you've eaten before it's too late.

In the interrogation block, your efforts to save yourself exist alongside another preoccupation, which is to escape the putrid odor that has clung to you since your first day inside that vault. That stench has a remarkable story, which each detainee tells in their own way, and it replicates ad infinitum. At that time, I would have fought to the death for an opportunity to take a shower and cleanse myself from the odor that had taken root in my nostrils. I needed to discover, after bathing and putting my clothes back on, whether my sense of smell would return unimpaired. Deep shame flooded over me each time the interrogator expressed his loathing for me and my smell. Neither multifarious beatings nor vituperation expressed in the vilest of words, nor even the smell of death that filled that place, could succeed in prodding my humanity out of its slumber. What did it was my own putrid stench, the feeling of disgust it produced inside me, and my shame in a place where shame is the least of your concerns.

In the interrogation block, they build a wall of ignorance around you, cutting you off from all sense of direction. They shake you like a pair of dice until constant dizziness sets in and makes it impossible to sleep, even though you have never been more tired.

In the interrogation block, you rebuild your relationships with your Lord and all your faiths. The pain might bring you to the point of calling upon God one last time, before faith and belief depart for good.

In the interrogation block, the changing of the seasons no longer holds meaning. Nor the rising of the sun, nor when it is blotted out. Such things ceased to occur when the walls closed in upon you.

In the interrogation block, you are the smell of your sweat, the taste of your brokenness, and prey to your own thoughts. You are an old copy of a document made up of notes with your signature scrawled at the end in hesitant letters.

In the interrogation block, you are everything, and nothing is yours.

Confession

"Confession is betrayal." That is one of the ugliest and most repugnant proverbs of our Palestinian struggle. A premature, absolute, and heedless judgment. Found within romantic, revolutionary orations written in a language from beyond the spectrum of pain, it is a judgment passed by those who have not choked on the smell of rusty iron. A judgment that flays you mercilessly, weighs down your spirit, and magnifies the assault of the barraging questions. A judgment that ignores your bleeding flesh, your halting breaths, the limitations of your faith, and your unbearably fetid odor. A judgment that drives you out of your dark Middle Ages into a Renaissance that no longer bestows forgiveness after a confession. Inside a church that stopped granting indulgences one hour before your birth, Michelangelo's angels watch your condemnation, pointing accusatory fingers and ready to pounce.

The scene is nearly deserted. You sit on your confessional chair, embraced by the smell of a kind of coffee that is foreign to your sharp Eastern palate. You begin to sip the coffee as though it is the last thing you will ever drink. The smoke of a cigarette rewards your cooperation and your candor after a month when only the beatings you endured kept you warm.

Phrases like "if you please" and "take your time" and "do you want another cup of coffee" come from nearby voices that, only hours before, were disgusted by your proximity. You hear an invitation to take a break if that will ease the trembling in your fingers as you write the first shaky words. Then you begin again, writing about your recent past and your distant past, and everything you did in each that would condemn you. You go on to write other things that would condemn you even more, and you are forced to leave out everything that would exonerate you.

Or that's what you think you were doing, up until the moment you are led back to your cell and the door is slammed behind you. You are surprised to discover that you wrote a confession and offered the evidence they needed to convict not only your past but also your tomorrow and every day after that. You realize that from the beginning the man with the questions was only interested in what you might do in the future, not what you had actually done, and that he was putting your future on trial, now that your past had slipped away from him. You also discover that you confessed to all the things that are going to happen to you: how you sleep, how many hours of shade you get during the heat of summer, the number of raindrops that hit you, your mood at the start of the day, the color of your toothbrush, the number of kisses and dates you will miss, your mother's age when the first wrinkles appear on her face, the first time your wife takes a second look at another man, which of your children will be the first to curse your absence, which of them will be the first to curse you.

Your interrogation ends by writing out things that you no longer care whether they were done by your right hand or your left. Precise translations of the languages used in the final report no longer interest you. Instead, your greatest effort is directed toward gaining a new understanding of yourself. You need to regain your ability to confirm directions, the position of the sun, the location of your shadow, the names and faces of those you love and those you reluctantly hate, the number of days in the week, your birth date, and which parent you feel closer to.

Then your self-examination begins, and all at once, you pose the questions you have been putting off, for this may be the very last time you'll get to ask. Is this the end? Which of your faults weighs most heavily upon you? How many times have you said "I love you" to your mother and really meant it? Exactly how idiotic were you for declining an alcoholic drink as you debated whether it was halal or haram? When will you next get an erection, and do you remember the last time? Which of your friends misses you most, and do you really care? The questions suddenly end. Your doubt contracts within you, replaced by a faith containing various identities and beliefs. Do any of them contain the forgiveness that will deliver you from the evil your hand has written? Acceptance and tolerance surge within you.

Things don't stop there. Indeed, acceptance continues expanding within, as testified by the many hours I spent in the company of small insects that began wandering through my cell with the confidence of those who know their way around in the dark and fear no danger to their lives. I became used to their gentle, lazy presence, a coexistence that—just a few months earlier—would only have lasted if I were too lazy to crush them in the corner of my room by any means necessary.

I don't think Freud would have bought this explanation of mine about those creatures. I think he would have dug deep into the events and happenings of recent months. He would have organized a meeting between me, my fears, and my ideas inside that cell of mine, in the company of the small creatures. Training his eyes upon my condition with that singular look of his during a psychological analysis, he would have come out with the following: "Is your tolerance and capaciousness of heart under such conditions truly what led you to do that? Or was the thing that saved those creatures your need for creatures weaker than yourself who would restore something you lost while hanging from the walls of that place: your need for power, which you feel when holding the life or death of another in your hands? After you've been crushed and broken, you need creatures whose wretchedness exceeds your own."

It's true. We do not perceive our hidden wells of strength without encountering some weaker being who points them out with their own feeble hand, fearing some violence that might erupt within us. How many times have the misfortunes of others comforted us and eased the abomination of our tragedies, only because they were bigger and more hideous than our own pain? And everything we said about solidarity, the universality of pain, and the globalization of oppression? Was that a consolation we only needed yesterday?

Thank God that Freud was not one of the things I read in that early stage of my life. It would have made things even more complicated, which was the last thing I needed.

My interrogation ended, and there was no longer any need for my presence in that dim cellar where I hung upon the walls. A crowd of iron vehicles was arriving, tasked with hanging up so many others, and the interrogators needed every vacancy upon those walls. There was already enough in my confession to guarantee a sentence of life in prison, enclosed by other walls in some other confining place. I spent my final hours there contemplating my black wall, as though discovering for the first time the only thing I could rely upon. I searched it for any natural affinity that suggested we were destined to be reunited and restored to a long partnership. Even at the time, I knew such a goal would never be realized unless I clung to that wall, holding fast to it as though there were nothing else I could rely upon. Even though it meant the rupture of all my former certainties, I would let go of everything that lay beyond it. I let go of the current answers and embraced unknown questions. I let go of Natalie's ice cream and held fast to small, empty bowls filled with possibilities. I let go of the girl who ignored me and held fast to the prospect of some other girl pretending not to know me. I let go of the me I knew and held fast to the one I was getting to know. I relinquished the world that had been my home and embraced the one where I now lived.

For the first time in months, I stood up straight and faced the wall. With a small, cold piece of metal, I began to carve two words that have accompanied me for the past twenty-seven years. Two final words that had not yet been uttered: Farewell, world!

Solitary Confinement

Don't set your roots too deep in any world you inhabit. That only makes the pain worse when they are torn out. When your time comes to be uprooted, live only upon the surface of this life. Don't extend your roots deeper by overprizing the things in your life, for if you can manage to rise above them, your essence goes beyond those things.

I did not speak many words of farewell when I departed the world I used to inhabit. But I spoke many words in the process of becoming reconciled with the wall they hung me upon, a wall that consumed one-third of my weight in the previous months and had an appetite for even more. Without casting a final glance to review the legacy I was leaving behind, I just waited for whatever surprises were to come in my new existence. I forgave myself all my mistakes, for prison, like faith, erases all that came before. I did not write out my advice for the future inmates, and apart from my two words, I left the rest of the wall's black space untouched for whoever would come after me, for prison, like drowning, is a unique and solitary experience: everyone enters it in their own way, and nothing can prepare you for breathing your lungs full of water except the experience of breathing your lungs full of water.

The interrogators did not give up on me entirely. After they finished picking my pockets of everything that interested them, along with other things they hadn't yet made up their minds about, they urged the necessity of moving me into solitary confinement and delaying my transfer—the normal next step—to one of the countless prisons that dotted the entire landscape of Palestine. They did so on the pretense that I still posed a risk to their dreams. They needed to quash any remaining revolutionary ideas I had built upon the legends of freedom and return.

The iron beast of a transport vehicle was called the busta. By peering through the small holes drilled into its metal sides, I could tell that it was still early spring. I did not steal many such glances because I was focused upon other holes inside myself, through which I reviewed the chaos of questions and semi-answers I was leaving behind. Indeed, I was eagerly awaiting our destination and a return to my wall, with the clarity of all its empty space and the profusion of questions and answers as of yet unwritten, since they would all come from me. I was the space where they operated. I was their doubt and their certainty. I was that boy who leapt from his wall so that he could dwell within it. On the other side of the busta's holes was my old form of hanging in the camp: my marginality, the alienation of place, the constraints of daily life, and people who abandoned their faith after a wave of new orations announced imminent measures to rescue their imitation cities from a dubious existence so they might become complete once again. Measures that would bar the gates of our cemeteries and permit us to die of old age.

I grew nervous at hearing the sympathy expressed by some of the detainees riding with me in the busta when they learned I was headed for the solitary confinement block in a prison located in the occupied city of Ramla, right in the center of Palestine. They seemed to know something I didn't, but I didn't ask. I was ready for whatever was to come. My pages were blank, ready to receive all manner of writing, in any color I wished, using any alphabet I chose. No one would dictate his articles of faith to me, the gods he worshipped, or the half-truths with which he stained the walls around him. This was my birth. I was the one who would choose my first cry, my first steps, and my first words, to whom they were spoken and how. I would choose which direction I'd look to find my wall. I was the one who would remove its ambiguity, obscurity, and doubt.

I was all my coming hours and all my seasons that were late to arrive. There was no longer any ocean that could swallow me, for I was master of the oceans, both the surface and the deep. I was master of the vault. There were no bonds that could shackle me. Things are what we want them to be. I would dwell in the heart of that place, even while floating upon its surface. I would tell its story in my own way. No roots would entangle my feet if I wished to soar through the air and come back down after losing all sense of direction. I would not hate the jailer nor what he believes about the doors he is locking. Hatred is nothing but a waste of energy and yet another lock. There is no door except the one I close upon myself.

Voices reverberated through the busta, and I noticed the proliferation of languages. Someone was grumbling in Arabic about the crowding. Another began crying out in the same language for the soldiers to loosen his handcuffs, which had been snapped too tight around his wrists. A third was threatening to wet himself if the soldiers continued to ignore his need to relieve himself. Another spoke in an Eastern dialect of Hebrew, which had lived so long on the margins of the Westernized Zionist project that it despaired of being accepted and began stealing from it. The last tongue was Russian, and it rose sharply against another prisoner over some minor thing.

When the tumult subsided, I returned to the many things I had resolved upon in order to prepare my frightened mind. The busta came to a stop at the prison entrance. After that was another stop, only a few dozen meters farther on, which brought us beside the entrance to the isolation block. Though I was shackled hand and foot, I was still able to descend a number of concrete stairs. At a gesture from one of the soldiers I turned to the right, and at another gesture I stopped. A door opened, a hand pushed me through, and the door closed behind me. The first day had begun.

At a depth of three meters, thirty-six cells shared a space that was roughly forty meters long and five meters wide. Each cell had two iron beds, one stacked above the other. Across from the beds was a place to bathe and perform other necessities. All this in a cell no larger than five square meters. How was it possible for such a concrete creature to exist? What decrepit hand designed it? What deaf hand constructed it? What fear gripped those in charge of it? What made them so afraid that they had to dig this tomb in which to hide the worst of their deeds and their terrors?

I looked around. Through the grate in my door, I saw exhausted faces of other prisoners that reminded me of myself. But when I hurried over to the small mirror hanging on the wall, I saw nothing I recognized on a surface corroded by the damp underground air and the complete absence of sunlight. I returned to look at the exhausted faces. The voices that took their place suggested the opposite of fatigue. Harsh, loud voices. Voices farther off joined the chorus. The characters, the voices, and what they were saying: all of it was very familiar. These were the lying gods. I hung from my cell door as they showered me with words of welcome. I clung there longer as they kept talking, still at it with all their lies. They fell silent after inviting me to catch my breath and make myself at home, but they promised to be back with me before long.

None of the details of that cell interested me. The only thing I cared about was the wall. My wall had stripped off the black garment of mourning it had worn in the interrogation block. Now it was dressed in a color that might have been white had it invested the least effort in removing the spots— so diverse in shape, color, and smell—that stained its body. The first thing I decided was that the two of us needed to wash, urgently and at length.

I stood in the middle of the cell, half naked, and stripped away everything that had taken place there before my arrival. I began to assign names to each of its features. The iron rack became a bed. The ceiling became blue and then more blue until it turned into a sky. The door with its metal bars evaporated: it was replaced by a hotel suite door, operated by a key card to keep out unexpected visitors. The wall was transformed into a document upon which I could compose all the texts I wanted.

While I was still giving things their names, the voices started up again with fiery declamations worthy of Trotsky. The lying gods would not have been able to persist with their lies in that vault had they planted deep roots in the soil and given up soaring high above the terrestrial realm. Only by breaking free from the pull of gravity could they promulgate their revolutions in that new space. Only by letting go of the idea of the cell door and the physical properties of iron could they grip their bars, strip the masks of fatigue from their faces, and pray for their revolutions.

The whole scene astonished me. The vault provided a depth and complexity that I desperately needed. I needed to enter a scene like that, which felt light-years away after my time in the interrogation block. I needed this scene of the lying gods with their tired faces and their energetic mouths to restore my balance and my faith. It was a scene that bridged two walls, the old one in the camp where I used to stand, preparing myself to leap, and this new one that I would jump onto, uncertain whether I could hold on. A few months in solitary confinement was exactly what I needed to systematize my relationship to the wall with calm deliberation, apart from any distractions. That would not have been possible had I been transferred immediately to one of the main prisons, crowded with hundreds of prisoners and thousands of stories—many of them similar but some contradictory—about the wall and life after the wall. I needed that short pause, alone and isolated, with a trio that would accompany me for the entire length of my journey: me, my Lord, and a most confining place. A holy trinity in its sanctum. Out of its lies, under its terror, above its sky, behind some disappointments and before others still to come, in its breast, lying in wait for it, close beside it, in its grave, in its truth, in its purpose: that was the space where I would write my exile.

When hearts are wounded, they crave solitude, either to heal in peace or else die. I saw souls that recovered and were healed despite the oppression of that place, the violence of its construction, the inhuman torture it inflicted, and a mistreatment that was daily and unceasing. I saw how those souls would depart their bodies in the morning and return only when the evening had begun, searching out any fresh wounds received that day. I saw them during their sole hour of sunlight in the paltry courtyard. Standing upon the hard ground, with barbed wire above, their eyes would light up as though catching sight of someone for the first time in a long, long while. I listened to their deep breaths inhaling the last rays of the sun as it passed from sight. I went down with them into the vault, their breasts now filled with enough life to sustain them until their next hour in the sun. I believed them when they said the sun rises at noon every day, just for them, and then disappears from this planet one hour later. Who can argue with gods whose Qur'an is a lie, whose religion is blind faith, and whose Sunna is pain?

My months in solitary confinement were a bridge between two worlds. During those months, I let go of my earthly alphabet and began to learn the language of the people of the sky, which allowed me to spin the old orations with new words. Those months taught me the sun's rarity, the shadow's care, and how spacious my narrow cell could be when I soared through it. I learned nighttime conversations and how to etch the wall with secrets I found under the corroded surface of the mirror. The water's turbidity, the wound's depth, medicine's scarcity, and a soul's ability to heal. The wonder of fantasy and the precise details of dreams. Trembling encounters with a woman on the edge of the imagination.

Then my months of solitary confinement came to an end. A few long meters away, the iron jaws of the busta opened with the threat of something new. All I could do was wait.

Starvation

I was not the only one to emerge from the solitary confinement block in the summer of 1993. In a space of less than two weeks, every single one of the detainees came out of isolation. Our book of Exodus was written by distant souls: all the prisoners scattered across the land, who united their diverse concerns to address shared causes.

After long and continual neglect on the part of the Occupation authorities, Palestinian prisoners became accustomed to join battle heroically by means of hunger strikes and other similar methods. That resistance movement witnessed numerous victories that improved their living conditions. Their occasional failures did not weaken the prisoners' resolve or dissuade them from repeating the attempts, time after time, despite the great cost in terms of the hunger and the patient suffering borne by victims and martyrs. Opposing the prisoners' protests was a merciless machine that possessed the necessary mechanisms of oppression, along with the social and political cover to go with it, that made the struggle to achieve their demands a matter of life or death.

Using old prisons left behind by the British Mandate authorities and building upon the ruins of the two Nakbas, the Occupying State constructed numerous prison camps that began to be filled after 1967 with young people whose social consciousness was not yet fully formed, even if their pain and feelings of loss were fully developed. These young people fought and were killed, or they fought and were cast into the gloom of the prisons. Inside those detention centers, Palestinian detainees suffered subjugation and abuse. They were disassociated from time and place after their actions were condemned by military tribunals that denied all international treaties and conventions, disdained international law, and adopted their own system of rules and laws in which condemnation remained the first and last judgment, without any consideration for justice. Inside those prisons, people could not long endure the misery of beatings, illness, stale air, and the deprivation of sunlight. Over the next several decades, prisoners engaged in many strikes, choosing to starve themselves under conditions that ranged from desperate to impossible.

For every need, there is a god before whom a person prostrates themself and promises sacrifices and vows of fealty should their need be met. Faith deepens if their god responds, while any delay or denial is met with a curse. Lucina, the goddess of pregnancy, aids in childbirth; Neptune is for sailors with tattered sails, lost at sea; Mars marches into battle beside warriors and becomes their sword should their own break in their hands. Meanwhile, monotheists have a Lord whose names, descriptions, and throne bearers change according to the need. During a hunger strike, the person starving possesses them all when their body begins to consume their own flesh and bones.

God, no longer a vast and distant idea, becomes closer to the starving person than their own breath, closer even than the imaginary meals they prepare every night to fill their bellies with an imaginary fullness. During a strike, all of God's names are forgotten, and words like One, Unique, Merciful, Vast, and Awesome no longer come to mind. Out of all the names and all their good, sweet promises that appeal to every aspect of the human mind, the only one that remains is Long-Suffering.

During a hunger strike, the body carries the spirit for the first ten days. After that, the roles are reversed, and the body becomes a heavy burden. During a strike, the only things that protect you from the night chill are the inflammation of your bowels, the fever of waiting, and embracing the wall. During a strike, your emaciated body no longer tempts beautiful women to visit your dreams when darkness falls. During a strike, your death comes to keep you company, and you keep watch over its breaths alongside you. Nothing comforts you except the passing of someone who slept on an iron bed nearby, which makes you resolve that you will not die as well. You sleep as close to the ground as your bones allow. You keep the water very close, within mouth's reach. You search in every direction for a qibla to orient your prayers. You prostrate yourself, but no ground receives your head. You give free rein to your hair, which is the only part of you that keeps growing. During a strike, you reject all the news that reaches you, and you only believe those who speak of victory.

The first hunger strike by Palestinian prisoners came in the year 1970. They did not achieve any significant progress to speak of, and during it, the prisoner Abdul Qader Abu al-Fahm was martyred. A similar strike took place in 1976. The third attempt, which came three years later, was sparked by conditions at Nafha Prison in the Negev Desert, where more than 150 prisoners were packed into small cells without any beds and were granted only one hour of outdoor sunlight per day. Their strike lasted twenty days, and three prisoners, Rasim Halaweh, Ali al-Ja'fari, and Ishaq Maragheh, achieved martyrdom when Occupation authorities insisted on force-feeding them. The prisoners achieved important gains: beds and mattresses were installed in the rooms, replacing the thin leather mats that had previously been spread on the floor. In addition, access to the sun in the courtyards of the cellblocks was increased and given a regular schedule. The achievements of that strike increased the prisoners' confidence in their ability to realize further improvements to their living conditions. In 1984, a new strike was announced that ended with many advances, the most important of which was the introduction of transistor radios into the rooms, permission for families to deliver pajamas and athletic clothing, and a greater quantity and variety of food.

After that, the prisoners lived several relatively quiet years until Occupation authorities announced a state of emergency inside the prisons when the first Gulf War broke out. Upon the conclusion of that war, the prison administration refused to restore prewar conditions, a decision that led the prisoners to launch a hunger strike that continued for twenty days. That strike ended with several improvements, in addition to the proclamation that the solitary confinement blocks, including the one where I was imprisoned, would be closed and all the prisoners confined there would be moved to other prison camps.

With steps made heavy by the chains around my ankles, I made my way out the door of the isolation block—or the vault, as I liked to call it. More than once, I paused to look back. My hesitation provoked looks of amazement upon the faces of the soldiers who served as prison guards. They began to urge me along with shouts and sometimes a shove. I do not know what irritated them more, that I was escaping from the vault or that I demonstrated a deep longing for it. From inside the busta, I looked at the solitary confinement block for the last time. A sudden fear came over me as I was struck by the reality of leaving my solitude and the damp evenings, leaving my wall and the few white surfaces I still had left there. I remembered the single hour of sunshine, and how my body would tremble as the warm touch of the sun's first ray played over my skin. In that isolation, there was something that resembled the days when I used to stand at the edge of the camp in the cool evening damp, finding a place outside a society that shackled everything I yearned for: I, the one who rebelled against the tribe's morality; I, the one with the strange questions, the one who stubbornly insisted on an answer.

The soldiers checked our bonds, our names, and our numbers, and after they confirmed that our naked bodies concealed nothing suspicious that might interrupt the progress of the convoy, the busta set in motion. Tension appeared on the faces of the other souls there with me. With a deep anxiety born from ignorance, everyone asked what was happening. The fear also mounted within me as I recalled what I had heard of overcrowded prisons, and how more than fifteen prisoners could be packed into a single narrow room. In such a press of bodies, without a space of my own, I feared for my relationship with my wall. I feared for my solitary hours at the beginning of each evening, and the desire of my nighttime visitors to have me all to themselves. I feared for my names and descriptions for things in an environment where everyone knew a thing and gave it a name of his own, possibly without leaving me space to do the same. What would happen to the decisions I made in my isolation about letting go, hanging upon the wall, and existing in time and place?

I was saved from this endless stream of questions by the busta's sudden stop, which launched our bodies off their seats and into the iron walls. Everyone cried out, and the commotion drew an even louder shout from our guards, who threatened harsh punishment if we did not immediately shut up. All the voices fell silent after a few minutes, but it was due to fatigue, not the threats. Over the next forty-five minutes that separated us from our final stop at the prison in Ashkelon, my tension and fear kept rising.

Now, as I write these lines, the time is 5:00 p.m. on Wednesday, the sixth of February, 2019. We have just received news of the martyrdom of Faris Baroud, a prisoner at the desert prison of Rimon, where he spent nearly thirty years after receiving a life sentence. Inside the iron beast of the busta all those years ago, this martyr, Faris, was sitting only two meters away from me, and I can still hear the sound of his cry when he unexpectedly slammed into the iron wall. *Faris* means "knight," and his name reminds me of the story of Asma bin Abi Bakr, that noble Arab woman from the dawn of Islam who went to the unjust ruler and pleaded for the body of her son, which was hanging on a gibbet. "Isn't it time for this *faris* to dismount?" she said. Now another knight has come down from his wall, after having clung there for so long. Faris's heart could not endure all this tumult. He tried to reconcile his relationship with prison more than once. After each failed attempt, he tried again. With each failure, he would escape voluntarily to solitary confinement—to the first wall, to the beginning of the wall. A quarter century has passed since we last met, and another quarter century might elapse before I go to join him at another wall, when another hour of sunlight shines down upon a final cry…

Take all your iron beasts, Faris, and bury them deep with you. Take with you the cigarette you shared with me when cigarettes had become scarce. Take your rough, leonine voice. Take our heavy spirits and the cool damp of Ramla. Take our contraband packing twine. Bring with you everything we forgot to carry and everything that was too heavy for us. Bring all the memories you have left of your mother, before and after she passed away. Bring the coast, home to both camp and sea. O refugee, bring a map of the house and all the old stories you remember. Bring your grandfather's key. Don't entrust it to us, for we no longer strive the way we used to. Take what you want, and choose for yourself any paradise you please. Now that you are gone, we have the wall, the long wall.

I will finish this story for the sake of Faris and for all the noble Farises who came before, as well as for the knights who have not yet dismounted from their walls. I will finish this story for others who have not mastered the arts of the wall, how to hang upon it and escape by clinging to it, such that they might learn from it and absorb its tears and its lessons. For every wall has a story, and that story is someone's to tell. Each of those people has a world, both vast and constrained.

They each have a vocabulary. They have partial things and other things that are whole. Each has a pain and a time of waiting. Each has the right to tell their story. Writing is a kind of healing, an open expanse of time. Writing is all the clear spaces that the world denies you, upon which you compose the lines in any language you choose.

We reached the prison at Ashkelon, the source of my tension and fear. Three-quarters of an hour separated two walls: one that I carried and one that carried me. Both of them are me.

Ashkelon

The busta came to a stop outside an old Ashkelon building. The smell of the sea filled the air, and its humidity had a different flavor than the one in my damp vault. Tall palm trees, bare of any dates, encircled the building a few meters from its walls. After a short pause, the wall opened its wide mouth and swallowed us. After a few more minutes of waiting, the busta finally disgorged its load. A cell door opened. We were all squeezed inside, and the door clanged shut behind us. Next came a damp and tedious waiting. The door opened a second time and what followed were individual, naked exhibitions as each body was searched. We all gave a solo performance in front of an officer who asked each of us about our intentions for the coming years. What answer could we give when we had no ambition at all beyond bathing and sleeping for an hour or more? Our performances ended without convincing the audience or winning any applause.

After a short procession, another door opened to reveal an open space beyond. It was a prison yard, boxed in by four concrete walls reaching up to a height of two stories on three of the four sides. (In total, there were five detention blocks, holding more than four hundred prisoners.) Upon entering the yard, the first thing that captures your attention are three trees: a tall palm tree in the center, bearing no fruit and casting no shade; to its left, a blossoming tree that provided a significant amount of shade; and to its right an acacia with a modest amount of shade—but very modest indeed. I stood for a few moments, taking it all in. Compared with my former vault, the sense of space astounded me, as did the number of people moving around inside: dozens of prisoners in groups of no more than five, walking in counterclockwise circles.

After a few minutes, I found myself inside one of the rooms. Seven beds were bunked above seven others. There was a small bathroom. A wooden table with four plastic chairs. Souls in motion everywhere: one washing, one cooking, another yawning, two shouting at each other across a new backgammon board. Then a person with a touch of authority in his voice was directing me to my bed. As I began arranging my things, all the activity suddenly ceased, even the shouting. Words of welcome and a few long embraces. Then everyone went back to what they had been doing. The person with the leader's voice was giving me information about the rest of the souls while helping me organize my bed. Then everything was finished. I was on a top bunk, right next to a window made of concrete and iron that looked out into the yard. A television was mounted on the opposite wall. Someone was sleeping a half foot away from my head. The first evening began.

I sat on my bed, watching everything and trying to take in the enormous amount of activity around me. I leaned my head against the wall and thanked God it was there, and that my head didn't fall through into empty space. It was a Thursday. Dinner was ready. Fourteen souls came together in the center of the room, forming a circle around dishes distributed across the floor. Everyone sat or squatted, each in his own way, some of which were strange, while others were funny, though I didn't laugh. We ate, and then people worked together to wash the dishes and clean and organize the room. The man with the assured voice invited me to sit with him, and he explained at length and in great detail how tomorrow would start and what the rest of my day would be like, all the things I had to do, what to avoid, and which actions were forbidden. He explained the time I would wake up and when breakfast was served. Our hours in the sunshine and the precise arrangements of the schedule. When I would read and sometimes even what. Where, when, how, and all the other questions, up until the time for going to sleep. So much information in one evening!

More friendly words accompanied my steps back to my bunk, where I found the window upon which I would fix many hopes during the coming nights when I stayed up late. Everyone went back to their own cares, allowing me the chance to be alone and digest my new situation. Each corner held a story. One guy talked about a book he was reading as another listened intently. Another guy was making a pot of mint tea, while a group nearby watched the soccer match. A guy in his fifties was reciting what seemed to be a poem. It contained many words that he paused to explain. The night was long in coming, up there near the ceiling, and I was exhausted by the wait. Down in the vault, where night came with the suddenness of lights being turned off, there was nothing to wait for. But now the darkness took so long to fall I thought it must have gotten held up along the way. If only it would arrive, so that no one would notice when my solitary night dialogues began, along with my first writings upon the wall!

Lying on my top bunk and staring at the ceiling two meters above, I began to review the landscape I had entered. I compared it to my experience of entering another city years before. I mean, my conscious entry into that place beyond the camp's walls, my close and detailed examination of things and faces and disparate time scales present amid the languages and dialects that crowded the scene. There was nothing in the Messiah's city that reminded you of a city. All its roads—the ancient alleys and side streets too—led to Maryam and the story in the Qur'an about her holding on to the palm tree. Even the chaos of people and the jumbled mix of colors. All of it pointed to Maryam, to her son, and to a church caught between two other religions: one that came earlier and denied the child, and a second that came later and expressed its goodwill toward that infant. That city told the exact same story in all the languages, with the modification of certain minor details or an addition here and there. The city was enveloped by villages, and by a camp that appeared and clung to its margins, fearing to be swept away. My young senses were at a loss to organize those disparate elements into one clear image. The situation demanded repeated visits, and many failed attempts to put it in order until I finally acknowledged the futility of an impossible task.

Ashkelon Prison felt just like my explorations of Bethlehem. That was the first conclusion I drew while lying upon my iron bed. It was not at all like that of my narrow solitary confinement. It was hardly a prison at all. All paths led to the courtyard with a palm tree in the center. People gathered within its walls from imitation cities, villages, and camps, in addition to others who came from beyond the sea, searching for a country they read about in newspapers from Beirut and the other Arab capitals, or a country they heard about in bedtime stories from mothers and grandmothers.

It was a familiar scene. I reassured myself that I would be able to integrate myself quickly, for I was surrounded by the lying gods, whose discourses I had learned by heart. Meanwhile, beside me I had the wall I brought with me, while moisture from the sea air filled my lungs.

I'd spend an entire year in Ashkelon Prison. There I learned the remarkable progression of a prisoner's relationship with routine. That relationship begins with profound hostility toward the monotony of events recurring with tedious regularity. The prisoner makes childish attempts to break a routine that he senses is getting closer and closer and threatens to swallow him up. Perhaps he wakes up an hour before or after his usual schedule. He puts off shaving for two days or so. He takes a longer or a shorter shower. He swaps his normal brand of cigarettes for another. He takes down one picture of his mother from his wall and puts up a second that is more cheerful. He skips his hour of outdoor sunshine one morning and suddenly decides to lose weight for the sake of his health. He shaves off a mustache that he's never before allowed even to be trimmed. The prisoner continues skirmishing with all his daily routines until the day comes when he calls upon God to save him from the demons that are driving him mad. The prisoner begins exhibiting the same zeal for the monotony of his day and his possessions that a writer feels for his text. Any disturbance to the schedule, any neighbor who wakes him up fifteen minutes early, could cause some psychological imbalance or harm to his circulatory system. A prisoner's reconciliation with routine might come sooner, or it might come later, but it inevitably arrives.

In Ashkelon, I would learn to write with small, cramped letters to avoid disturbing my neighbors. I would learn to sleep through the sound of intermittent snoring. To wait patiently for the toilet, even if ten others were patiently waiting their turn ahead of me. To pretend to sleep, even while knowing that many sleepless hours lay ahead. To listen to more than one story at a time, ready to answer any sudden question meant to test whether I was paying attention. To pray with the others and add my amen to every supplication, even when I didn't agree. To pray for God to grant the cook a long life, even if his food ruined my appetite for the coming week. To wash my entire body with the smallest possible amount of warm water so that the next person in line would be spared a sudden jet of cold, and I would be spared his muttered imprecations. To walk in unison with seventy others, moving steadily in a circle without getting dizzy.

In that year of mine, I would also learn the limitations of my correctness and the probability of being wrong. Learn how to temper my rebelliousness, if only a little. To surrender to the views of the collective, even when it was wrong. To ask God's pardon constantly, without any particular reason, and to praise God for everything. To receive every newcomer as though he were the last. To sit in silence with someone who weeps for a father who has passed away before his time, or someone who curses a loss that has come too soon. To wait for the first cup of coffee that would start my day as I read Russian or Soviet literature. I learned to bid farewell to those whose walls grew tired of holding them, and so have set them free. I learned to relinquish my isolation and to hold fast to whatever opportunities for solitude I might steal.

In Ashkelon, I saw people who were in prison and yet were soaring. I saw faces leave their trace upon a mirror from how intensely they gazed into it. I saw the lying gods, who continued their transgression of believing, crediting, and writing their slogans, just as they kept distributing their monthly pamphlets and calling for the revolution. I saw them express unending solidarity with all the proliferating pains of the world, tending and caring for each pain like a prisoner who tends the dervish of hope. They expressed solidarity with the poor of the world by delaying or even sending back meals on their behalf. They expressed solidarity with workers and with peasant farmers, raising their voices with them to pray for rain. They expressed solidarity with women in the face of a patriarchy that oppresses both individuals and societies.

I spent my first days observing and learning. Watching and listening more than I spoke, I analyzed and interpreted the behaviors of the souls around me. Abruptly, at the end of my first week, I saw souls donning their bodies as though for the first time. They took stock of themselves and confirmed that every part was in its place, that nothing was missing or damaged. It was a Tuesday: the day before the visit.

The Visit

On Wednesday morning, everything changed. People woke to bodies that began to shake off the cobwebs of two weeks of fitful slumber in dark corners. They sought ways to hide a wound still healing after their latest brawl, or the lingering signs of an illness. The entire scene underwent a transformation as I lay on my bed, surprised and baffled by the speed with which everything changed.

In our room were ten Gazans who had grown up by the sea, their skin darkened by the salt water and the sun's slow transit over the suffering contained within that narrow, over-crowded strip of land. Ten souls who slept half the night and then spent the remaining half in a vigil for the morning. Ten souls who prayed that heaven would stay up late or else rise early enough to travel alongside buses carrying the scent of the sea folded inside their sisters' small handkerchiefs. Buses carrying a mother's supplication, hidden from her other children when she rose two hours before dawn to wrap her prayers deep within her clothes. The mothers check to make sure it is there and add a few more pleading words. They check a third time with even more pleading. Buses carrying children who have lost hope after standing for hours before a picture, a mute picture, whose silence offers nothing to quench a burning thirst, nothing to feed an aching hunger, nothing to answer repeated questions about a father's absence.

I kept observing the activity around me on that strange morning. People crowded in front of our single mirror. One of them shaved, and another checked his already shaved face. A third tried to stanch the trickling results of shaving too fast, while a fourth lost his patience and urged them all to get out of the way. After shaving, the next stop was the shower. Everyone sat on his bed, wrapped in layers of tense anticipation along with clothes that had been washed with exceptional care. After every shower was concluded, people called out the typical greeting—"Na'eeman!"—followed by pointed remarks about the possibility of going faster when others are waiting. A new round of crowding around the mirror to comb their hair and check once more on their shave. In the absence of any perfume, they moisturized their faces with burning eau de cologne. There were bantering remarks about everyone finally being ready, followed by some last visits to the mirror or to a suitcase. Someone made another pot of coffee, using the flames to consume a few of the long minutes that oppressed his nerves. The smell of cigarettes filled the room, along with clouds of anxious smoke. Someone kept asking why the list of visitors was taking so long. He asked again, and no one had any reply to reassure him. At ten o'clock the list finally arrived. The gods watching over the journey from Gaza had answered the prayers of those who had spent the night praying until they were too tired to pray any longer and collapsed in sleep.

Another week went by before it was my turn to pray and pray until I fell asleep midprayer. The morning brought a shower, coffee, endless cigarette smoke rolling across the ceiling, and an answer from the gods of the longer journey from the West Bank, whom I had weighed down with pleas and invocations. The buses carried mothers, wives, children, brothers, sisters, grandmothers, fathers, and grandfathers. Friends, both male and female, and on rare occasions, lovers, both male and female... Buses that carried news, stories, desires, and reproofs for a long separation. They carried despair and unalterable anguish. They carried four seasons of clothes together with the destitution of poverty.

Setting off at the break of dawn, those buses carried an emotion through lost birthplaces, through the ruins of houses and cemeteries of abandoned villages, where the dwelling places of the living and the dead were never far apart. Driving among those ruins, the buses carried the emotion across a temporal bridge that reunited, for a few hours at least, the distinct cultural moments separated by the Nakba of 1948 and the Naksa of 1967. Every geography associated with a memory remains fixed, unmoving. When we return to our pain, we return not to the geography of the pain but to that moment in time. We feel that pain again, and it could be taking place on a different planet. For all we know, the place might have changed completely, dressing the pain in a new topography, foreign and unfamiliar. But the time of the pain remains unaltered. Having been deprived of the geography of each catastrophe, their time remains present within us always.

The buses journeyed through the ruins of older pains until they reached the most recent ones. Mothers and grandmothers let the children exit the bus first. Last came the wives, who sat in the back and checked their faces in small mirrors, paying no attention to their children or their mothers-in-law. Once everyone was out, they were divided into groups that matched the number of chairs in the visitation room. Then they passed through a small and well-lit inspection room, one for men and another for women, an ordeal that would not be mentioned in the coming hours.

In my room, a cup of coffee and a cigarette accompanied the final minutes of the wait. A door opened. There was a very slight descent in the company of guards. We had our own physical inspection, the details of which did not differ much from the experience on the other side. We entered the visitation room. A careful search of the faces seated across a grate composed of small metal squares that were just large enough for halves of fingers or the edge of a kiss. Behind those squares sat my mother and the relatives who came with her. "Hello, my dear! How are you, my child? God willing, you're okay?" Half kisses, fingers embracing between narrow iron squares. "I've missed you, my child! How are you? God willing, you're okay? Your health is good?" My mother repeated her questions, as though confirming my ability to lie. My mother would not have been able to survive a single honest answer to any of her questions. I'm good at such lies, and by believing them, my mother saved herself from going mad. She pulled at my fingertips in a kind of embrace, sometimes kissing them. "God willing, you're doing okay, my child? Your health is good? You're not sick at all, my child? Look, your brother bought you a new shirt, he sends his greetings...Did you have breakfast, my child? Are you getting enough food to eat? Yesterday, your sister cooked the grape leaves you like. She wished you were with her like in old times. Her children are driving her crazy, my child. Your eyes look tired. Why aren't you sleeping more, my dear?" She pulled harder on my fingers and kissed them again. Then my mother left the iron squares so that other fingertips might come to embrace mine and other lips come to kiss me.

My father stood apart until everyone else had taken a turn. My father hated all the talking. He gave my fingers a quick squeeze and asked about my health, ignoring my desire for him to remain close and to grip my fingers longer. That's how my father repaid me for ignoring all his advice that would have ensured my welfare and his own. My father never believed for a single day in the ability of the lying gods to deliver him from his pain, even though there was never a day when he prevented me from believing in them, or kept me from activities he was certain would end badly for me. My father moved back, resuming his former distance in silent pain. The small iron squares were taken over by the other fingertips, those of my sister who missed our nightly walks, when her arm held mine to keep from falling. The fingertips of a little brother who saw me as a god he wanted all to himself, at least until he grew older, when the questions came rushing in and he began searching for other gods who would not abandon him in his time of need.

"I'm fine. My health is good. I'm sleeping well. They give us so much to eat I get a stomachache. I pray regularly, with full faith and submission. Every night, the most beautiful women of the tribe fall asleep at my side. Every day I write poetry, passionate and hopeful. I don't care that the girl who used to ignore me has gotten engaged to a man I hated. You won't have to wait for me long, Mother. I'm even closer to you than the fear you feel for me. I hear what you are saying, Father. We'll get to go on many walks soon, Sister. Don't find some other guy to take my place!" And many other lies that my visitors wanted to believe. Some of the lies I had spun between my prayers, and others between the first cup of coffee and the last cigarette I lit that morning.

For three-quarters of an hour, my visitors wore faces free of any fatigue, and bodies that had not been violated by their silent passage through the physical inspection. After my first words, we all performed our roles well. None of us let slip a phrase or movement that made any concession to reality or betrayed our lies... For three-quarters of an hour, a prisoner once again became a father or a brother, a sister, a mother, a daughter, or a wife, a lover. For three-quarters of an hour, you believe all the words of love, and your heart dances to the melodies of your mother's old songs. For three-quarters of an hour you drop down off your wall, and you don't care how far you must fall. Nothing remains except the small iron squares and the burning of your fingers after each embrace. You forgive your eyes the sin of crying, and you pardon your limbs if they grow weak and fail you at the first encounter. Three-quarters of an hour that restore everything you have relinquished, only to take it all back when the time is up.

The visit was coming to an end, or so we gathered from the movements of the guards around us. There was general chaos on the other side of the grate. Everyone crowded together for the sake of a final embrace. Mothers clung to their sons' fingers, refusing to let them go. Who could tell if that was to be their very last embrace? Signs of relief appeared on the faces of children, for this bizarre scene would soon end and they could go back to the games they understood. An imprisoned father pleads for a last kiss from a son who hides behind a mother's dress and wonders what this man with the unfamiliar face behind the iron squares wants from him. A teenage girl, wearing more clothes than necessary to conceal the forbidden fruit growing upon her body, stands across from a father who now hesitates to kiss her goodbye. A wife, not yet in her forties, takes advantage of the confusion to steal a glancing kiss or several, something that might put out the fire ignited every night by the empty half of her bed.

My mother gave me some final advice before she set my fingers free: "Sleep well, my child. Be sure to eat! Don't worry about us. We are fine. There's nothing we need except for you to be with us. My dear child, the beloved of my life, take care of yourself!" That's what my mother called me, the beloved of her life. Then she released me, and I embraced the other visitors with the fingers she gave back. My father kept standing apart and waited till the end. He gave me a cold embrace and then abruptly broke away. Families began to exit the visitation room. Bodies moved toward the door while their eyes lingered behind. My fingers remained twisted through the small metal squares. The last thing I saw was the hem of my mother's dress.

When they were gone, silence took their place. Our half smiles. Traces of tears. Confused faces looking up at the ceiling. Plastic bags with clothes filled with the scent of those who had been there. Then the guards returned, and I retraced the steps that would bring me back to my bed. For a while I lost myself in the news and events of the visit. Then I buried those forty-five minutes somewhere deep and inaccessible, and I went back to organizing my life as it had been before: my wall, the things people said about world affairs, some talk about the hereafter, the next time we'd get an hour outdoors, and my scribbling upon the wall.

The souls in prison continued with their activities and their interests, both internal and external, under a climate that hinted at sharp twists and turns ahead in their story. They closely observed everything that was occurring in the public squares of Palestine and around the world, and how those developments contributed to the slow death that was strangling their revolution. Until, that is, some Palestinians surprised the world with a rich political meal they had secretly cooked up in the Michelin-starred restaurants of Europe.

Oslo

At the start of the 1990s, in a world turning upon a single axis, all the powers of darkness and light came together for a shared purpose. Supported by regional centers, semi-states, statelets, and local organizations, they concocted every possible scheme to extinguish a single spark. The Intifada of the Stones had ignited a spark of faith, a belief that things were possible if we wanted them to be so. That's why we fought our little wars. That's why we were killed and buried. Or were killed and went unburied. That's why we were chased and pursued and clapped in irons, disappearing into more than one vault and many different prisons.

In September 1993, when some representatives of the Palestinian people met with the leaders of the Occupying State and signed an interim agreement called the Oslo Accords, the prison camps rose to their feet and remained standing. Political roundtables, convened in small rooms, lasted for months. Leaders among the prisoners moved heaven and earth to interpret and justify the momentous event as its details began to percolate among us. Factions arose, for nothing that was happening resembled the lying gods or their lies. Some voices rose in opposition. A feverish race began for the full details of the story and the right to be the one to tell it.

Nothing blunts a lie like a bigger lie. The architects of Oslo had nothing to offer apart from small lies about a fragmented story. They were storytellers who did not believe the happy endings of their own beautiful lies. They came riding in on black stallions that had nothing to do with us, and the steps they took were shorter even than our own halting breaths. They came wearing military uniforms unseen for a thousand years on the field of battle, or else civilian clothes unsuited for either the workshop or the fields. They came in moral and social organizations that still operated on a tribal basis, or else with a civilization so new that it belonged nowhere. They were demigods who dwelt in semi-legends, telling partial lies that they half believed and drawing sort-of maps for possible regions.

A prisoner cannot be saved except through the lies he believes. Some prisoners held fast to their old story, which they rewrote in even bigger letters and kept proclaiming loudly to avoid being pulled off the stage. Some prisoners cried out against traitors and infidels, pelting those false gods with seventy stones. They hung from their walls and waited, praying and fasting and beseeching the Lord of the worlds for an imminent deliverance. Other prisoners cried out against the traitors and their lies, but they did not denounce them as infidels since they didn't believe in hell to begin with. They too hung from their walls and waited, hoping that some good fortune might reach them out of all the lies and betrayals. A large portion of the prisoners wanted to believe. They hung from their walls and waited, some praying and fasting, while others were content just to hang and wait, justifying a new beginning with the old words they preserved in their memories and used to decorate their walls.

A new legend is only born when an old one dies—or when it is killed. Its falsehoods fall away from the walls, leaving no trace to remind us of it. Upon its ruins, the new storytellers construct another legend, either by force or by deception. They tell ever more presumptuous lies about Palestine: Palestine as the unifying bond, Palestine as the site of resurrection, Palestine as the land of God and the prophets. There is a Palestine of the stones, a Palestine of the sea and the sky, a Palestine of memory and old names. Palestine that relates to all, though nothing compares to it; Palestine that compensates for all, though nothing compensates for it. Palestine as my father choking up when he visits me. Palestine as the tears of all those who pray and also those who have abandoned their prayers. No sun outshines Palestine, while it gives shade to all... These were just a few of the scribbles that I began carefully inscribing upon my wall and the other walls where I wrote. The walls lacked the space for yet another story in need of commentaries, explanations, and justifications. The rough walls could not endure the slick semi-orations of a political narrative and regional and international conditions.

A cold winter lay ahead for the Palestinian prisoners, during which hearts were further divided. Some souls received new lies from the old prophets, who altered their message according to an updated revelation. Others clung even tighter to the texts of their old religion as they went on hanging from their walls. The prison yards closed in upon the souls. So did the cellblocks and their rooms. Only one story could fit within those contracting spaces. The lying gods scattered and plunged from their heaven to dwell in their desert. Poverty, hunger, and injustice were given multiple translations. Contrasting points of view about freedom and liberation proliferated. History and geography became muddled and jumbled within sensitive souls. Holy things were reversed, and everything that was haram became halal. Stories multiplied as storytellers contended and advanced their arguments from every possible angle. They pretended to forget their Nakbas. They pretended to forget the camp, the village, and the imitation cities. They pretended to forget the public squares that embraced them, the graveyards that accompanied them. After Oslo, life continued like that for the prisoners until the signing of the Cairo Agreement in May 1994, when the prison camps felt their walls shake to their very foundations.

The prisoners who had been in the camps since 1967 had witnessed numerous moments of liberation. Emancipation came for some, leaving the rest to pray for some future end to their suffering. Those opportunities were created by people exiled far from their homeland. Stubborn people who kept the faith and the creed. Across the previous decades, these opposition groups had signed numerous prisoner exchange deals. More than 150 Palestinian prisoners were freed in the 1970s. A prisoner exchange in 1983 liberated more than 5,000 Palestinian prisoners. The exchange of 1985 freed 1,150 prisoners, out of 2,500. The number of detainees in Israeli prison camps had dwindled to a few hundred by the end of 1987, when waves of mass detention during the Intifada of the Stones filled the camps with more than 12,000 prisoners by the beginning of 1994.

The signing of the Oslo Accords in September 1993 saw an initial flood of prisoners set free: all the sick and the minors. That step was followed by a pause until the Palestinian Liberation Organization and the Occupying State signed political agreements in Cairo the following May. The anticipation of those eight months awakened the hope of freedom, or at least the expectation of receiving a schedule for release. The month of May grew closer every day until it was at the very doorstep. For days, prisoners remained frozen in front of the television screen, following the news and waiting for the day when the Cairo Agreement would be ratified.

Life as we knew it came to a halt. The prisons, together with all the people and things they contained, hovered between land and sky. On rare occasions, they came down to attend to some earthly need. They ate, drank, or washed their bodies. Then they rose again, suspended and waiting. They slept on their feet. They ate without hunger. They parted from their walls as though the walls didn't exist. They postponed their stories and the various texts they used to argue about. They edged away from their legends, waiting to fall away from them entirely. They neglected their murals. They forgot their prayers and invocations. They got up in the night, unable to sleep, and smoked a cigarette. They went back to bed and didn't rise till late in the morning. They took out photo albums to make sure of the faces inside before hiding them away again. They searched their bags for the new clothes they were saving for the next visit.

The Chief Storyteller arrived in Cairo to sit down with the Occupying State and sign documents and maps he was unable to explain. Later, news of his inability reached the souls hanging in their rooms inside the prisons. Some deferred their criticism of Yasser Arafat and waited. Then the lists arrived with the names of the prisoners to be released, prepared in advance for the moment of the agreement's signing. An announcement came over the loudspeakers inside the prison: until the first group of names was read, everyone had to remain silent, as silent as the grave. Those whose names were read checked their voices and held their breath with constrained joy. When the first list was finished, those liberated names leapt and danced and embraced and kissed. They wept, made their farewells, and donned their new clothes. They wept and embraced a second time. Doors were opened, and those names departed from their walls.

Once again, the silence of the grave. A second group of names. Breathless waiting. The announcement was over. Dancing, jumping, embracing, kissing, crying, and a final farewell. Opened doors, and souls departing their walls. Then I was alone. I looked around me. Out of thirteen people, nothing was left behind except their final breaths, which circled through the air of our shared room. A strange smell of empty space, of silence, of nothingness took their place. Again I looked around. My face was coated by a riot of odors left behind by the kisses of those departing. I washed my face. I washed it a second time. I began repeating the names of those who had been there, counting them up. I forgot a name or two. I ran to the closed door. Nothing to be heard or seen. The silence of the grave. I returned to my bed and clung to the wall.

Some hands are clean, and others stained with blood. That is what the Chief Storyteller decided and signed his name to: no deliverance for anyone who went too far in his story or got too deep in his narrative, who raised his hand to cut off the sword that bereaved him. Arafat spun a new legend, with no room for the gods of war and their revolutionary speeches. It was an astonishing legend about gods of peace who had only been faking their old orations. Now they had tired of their exile and sought refuge with the first land that would take them in.

The prisoners of war returned with their gods to their walls, which remained just as they were: solid, fixed, and welcoming any writing etched upon them. The walls received their souls with open arms and promises to be there forever. Those souls returned and gathered together into a few rooms, now that the former ones were empty but for ghosts. The list of names cared nothing for their dreams, and the loudspeakers were silent about their pain. The doors had been slammed in their face. Returning from the middle ground in which they had been suspended, they abandoned all the romantic adventures they had begun planning, for all the promises had been a lie. They returned to their single fixed wall, a wall that was the beginning of the story, its middle, and its end.

I remained alone only for a few hours before I was transferred to Block No. 4, together with all the souls whose names went unspoken. We sat in silence a long time, avoiding words that would inflame an unassuageable pain merely by being uttered.

Fear

The cemetery, man's final resting place,
is the birthplace of the gods.

—LUDWIG FEUERBACH

When death becomes imminent, a long-smoldering fear of the unknown grows within us. Fear becomes our entire existence: what we believe, what we doubt, and what we think; our emotions and everything we feel; everything we failed to understand; the people who filled our hearts, and those who seeped out through the cracks; the steps we trod and the chances we lost; the words we said, those we hid, the ones we twisted.

In all the horizontal expanse of our lives, the only thing that can save us from the verticality of death is a firm faith in an afterlife and a belief in a god or gods, merciful and eternal. Just as bodies contorted by the cold huddle together around a flame, mortals coalesce around the idea of immortality. Life's meanings and goals stretch out in every direction, and we are tormented by a fear of abrupt endings. Fear amplifies the question of what comes after death, even as it reveals our ignorance of any answers. So we flee upward. We search for anything to hang on to, so as not to plunge back into the hell of questions and of fear. We never look down, for the abyss contains nothing but graves, absence, and the end.

Black clouds filled the sky over Ashkelon Prison. Under their persistent darkness, the remaining prisoners had to breathe, evaluate their situation, and renew old relationships with their walls. They were the first victims of the new story that emerged after Oslo; they would not be the last. These souls began lashing out at everyone they believed responsible for their continued captivity. They flayed them with vituperation, even calling them traitors. With their own hands, they planted the seeds of doubt and mistrust among beliefs that, until the day before, had been as firm and stable as the walls erected upon them.

My wall saved me when everything around me was in motion. Not for a single day did I doubt its ability to encompass and explain all the motion around me. I did not search for new gods. My wall already contained all the faith I needed. Other prisoners lost their points of stability and were carried any way the wind blew. Dizzy and sick, they lost confidence in the story of the land and a certain victory.

Upon a nearby wall hung other souls who, from the beginning, rejected the legend of the land. Instead, with all the certainty of faith, they adopted a story about heaven and the sayings of the prophets. Those souls did not possess a story that resembled them. Instead, they saw themselves as participants in a story prepared long ago, beyond the limits of the sky. Their history contained no defeats or setbacks, just various stages when they temporarily paused on their way to an imminent divine victory. They cared nothing for other people's stories and legends. They denied the other prophets and the demigods who spent half their lives in alleys, eating, drinking, bleeding, and dying. Those souls had all the answers. Questions no longer plagued them with doubts. After sleeping soundly upon the pillows of certainty, their dawn prayers suffered from no sleepless hours.

Such answers, I was certain, are shackles. They denied the yearning of the road and foreclosed the opportunity to search, hoping for some future arrival. All the same, when I found myself wandering through a maze of possibilities, I envied those souls. They slept the whole night through while I hovered at the edges of sleep. I was jealous of their single god and the shortcuts they found to reach Him. I was jealous of all the prophets and their stories, with guarantees of intercession and salvation. But my jealousy would always fade when a new question brought me back to the start of the road. Then I looked at those souls hanging upon their walls. They didn't possess any real faith in their God, no true belief. They just denied everything that came before Him or would come after. They hung from Him, fearing Him and desiring Him. They ignored all the ignorant scribbles that distorted their God's face. They left off writing entirely and broke their pens. Embracing a ready-made text, they merely carried out their Lord's first command in the Qur'an: Read.

That was how I spent the spring of 1994. After the Cairo Agreement in May, a new atmosphere descended upon Ashkelon. Uncertain souls sought some reason to justify their continued presence after the waves of prisoner releases. Other souls simply reverted to their previous existence. The Occupation authorities began to cede to the Palestinians the task of governing the main West Bank cities. I can still see Palestinian security forces and police entering Gaza, with people dancing and throwing sweets as they came to believe the news. Sitting in front of the small television screen, I couldn't believe it—refused to—and my eyes filled with tears. I cried the exhausted tears of one who wants to believe, if only for a short time, his own lies. Or maybe they were the tears of dreamers, afraid for their dreams lest some morning, false and colluding, come too quick and steal those dreams away. But still I cried to see it, and all my doubts couldn't stop me.

Spring ended, and summer came, bringing a new appointment with the iron beast. This time the busta would take me to the occupied city of Nablus, which had not yet been handed over to the Palestinians. Jnaid Prison had been built there in 1984, and in the first decade of its existence, its cellblocks devoured tens of thousands of West Bank detainees. Within its walls, both the leadership and the rank and file of the Palestinian nationalism movement had been born. I arrived in August and spent several weeks in Block No. 3 before being transferred to Block No. 7, where a new window offered me a magnificent view from the east side of the prison, overlooking the quiet and sleepy neighborhood of Rafidia.

The conditions within Jnaid Prison were no different from Ashkelon, but there was a sense of boiling excitement, liable to explode at any moment, which I came to understand derived from a greater consciousness of the political events that were taking place in the Palestinian public square. Fear had an entirely different nature in Jnaid. It was so close it almost burned your fingers. It was a familiar fear, something I had come across before. A fear I knew, and it knew me. Something in its taste and the tang of its scent reminded me of alcohol.

I was startled by the feeling that came from being trans-
ported. A transfer from one geography to another is neces-
sarily accompanied by a transformation in one's emotional
state. That is, every physical relocation takes place between
two emotional states, and likewise, between two cultural
moments, each representing its own unique mood. The Israeli
Occupation of 1948 imposed a cultural time that was different from the situation in the West Bank and the Gaza Strip,
lands that were only occupied in 1967. The first occupation
established a new state that abounded with the elements and
vocabulary of modernity, as much in its political organizations
as its social structures and civil planning. On the other hand,
the occupation that came in 1967 imposed a frozen temporal
state upon lands that saw no development or change, only the
plundering of all the natural resources they contained.

The geography of Palestine experienced the events of the
Occupation as a fundamental contradiction of its identity,
its nature, and its culture; of its sky, its air, and its mood; of
its language and its emotions. Moreover, the Israeli Occupation succeeded in creating two entirely different cultural
moments within a single small geography, which strained
under the extreme disparities. The 1967 lands existed with a
heavy Arabic tongue, scarce water, rudimentary agriculture,
pre-mechanical manufacturing, tribal and familial social
structures, plundered natural resources, and abject poverty.
It was a geography that diminished every hour as a result of
land confiscation policies pursued by successive governments
of the Occupation. On the other side was the land lost in
1948, with its strange Hebrew tongue, an abundance of water,
expansive land, advanced agriculture, modern factories based

on advanced technologies, and a democratic Jewish political entity based upon the principle of the citizen. That geography expanded every hour at the expense of the land in the West Bank. Nothing could satiate its appetite for plunder and confiscation.

A Palestinian experiences a state of temporal confusion on his land each time he moves between those two geographies. One is a space he knows. It resembles him in all the details captured within its old temporal bubble. It understands the deficiency of his resources and promises to provide him with enough if only he would be content and satisfied—even as it promises him more if only he resists and takes vengeance. The other space he doesn't know. It doesn't resemble him at all but kills him, robs him, and denies him. It promises to continue doing the same if only he would be content and satisfied—even as it promises him yet more oppression if he merely thinks about resistance and vengeance. The Occupying State possessed all the military might it needed, which it then crowned with nuclear capabilities. That is the language with which it speaks to Palestinians and the surrounding states.

The Palestinian has to hold fast to every god he knows and others he does not believe in. He has to fashion a crisis out of his poverty, his incapacity, and his ignorance of his Arabic environment. In the face of a monster that began growing in his land until it swallowed it up, a legend is the only thing he possesses. The task of the Palestinian is not easy in the face of a discourse that shakes all his articles of faith. His parallel time pursues him wherever he turns. One minute he calls upon God for a rainy winter to nourish the fields he still possesses; the next, he prays for all water to be withheld from the

land. He prays for a divine anger to come down and demol-
ish all that the Occupation has built upon his land, but the
moment his prayer ends, he begins to marvel at the genius
of what has been built. He strips any sense of legitimacy or
legality from the Occupying State, though its democracy and
its independent authority never cease to impress him. He
accuses it, blames it, and denounces it as criminal every time
he lies down to sleep or his harvest fails, yet he remains astonished at its remarkable capacities.

Every Palestinian tries with all his strength to ward off
the painful reality of two parallel times imposed upon his
land. No matter how much he tries to deny it, he recognizes
the physical and emotional transfer that occurs between two
geographies, and he confesses his alienation. On other occasions, he clings to his legend and its lies: that there is but a
single geography, always present everywhere, and a constant
emotional state that remains unchanged even when he is
moved from one place to another. He yells as loud as he can,
repeating his revolutionary discourse, with a few lover's words
added in. He listens carefully; he looks close. He excavates
his memory and recalls his time and place. He cries aloud a
second time: I am master of this place! I am the sea, the beach,
and the breaking of the waves. I am the sky, the air, and what
carries the birds. I am the plain, the meadow, and the flock of
pigeons. I am the sand, the kohl, and the springs of water. I am
the boulders, I am the eagle. I am the flower and the bee. I am
the partridge. I am the valley, the plain, and the coast. I am the
Old Man of the Mountain.

That's the emotional shift I was afraid to acknowledge
when I arrived in Jnaid Prison. It seemed that admitting such

a thing would constitute a betrayal and a surrender. It would mean believing the lie about a bifurcated land and two identities. It meant accepting the illusion of temporal and cultural distinctions between Ashkelon in the 1948 land and Nablus in the 1967 land. Entering the West Bank, I was afraid of my familiarity with the air, the smell, the arrangement of the houses, the voices of the soldiers that still filled the narrow streets of Nablus. In contrast to yesterday's exile in Ashkelon, I was frightened by the feeling that I was coming back to a place that resembled me.

But my fear passed. It did not come between me and my wall. I waited for the approach of night, when I could be alone with my wall and with the view of Rafidia generously offered by a window that just happened to match the level of my top-bunk bed. I made my coffee and sat cross-legged on my bed. I received the evening that spread over the streets of the neighborhood. Everything seemed close—everything except the faces, which were impossibly far away.

The Occupation authorities, which had not yet handed Nablus over to the Palestinians, were still pursuing their oppressive policies toward the inhabitants of the city. In the prison, we found cells that had witnessed scenes of interrogation and torture. From our rooms, we listened to the sound of gunfire coming from the direction of the demonstrations. The months of waiting and watching were interspersed with waves of prisoner releases like those seen in Ashkelon, though in smaller numbers. Those months were also interrupted by the hunger strike of May 1995, during which the prisoners articulated their clear reading of the political scene and the agreements that were making their pain permanent. They demanded that the Palestinian leadership hold fast to the principle of liberation for all the prisoners. On account of external interference and internal reactions, the strike ended after eighteen days without achieving any result.

Slow, heavy months passed for souls that hung upon their walls, overshadowed by news of the imminent transfer of the city to the Palestinians. Anxious about their fate, they published numerous letters to decision-makers on the Palestinian side. They suppressed the intense feelings of fear that possessed them, yet that fear remained present, lurking watchfully in every corner of the prison.

I would spend nearly one-and-a-half years at that window, directly across from a Nablus family whose small house was divided into a hundred or more small squares by the iron grate over my window. The scene never changed, and nothing altered its beauty and perfection. I experienced the details of daily life alongside that family. I woke in the morning with them, watching for the first light inside the house. A woman's face, expressionless, would light up a small kitchen and move around on short steps. Other lights awoke in the other corners of the home: two children came out its door on their way to school; a mother went up to the roof to hang laundry in the sun. After that, no motion disturbed the calm of that house.

After leaving my window for my daily routine, I would return and see military vehicles pursuing young people through the streets. Numerous other scenes recalled the details of a legend that had been absent from my mind for the past two years. I waited for the arrival of evening, when the inhabitants of that home would reassemble. Joining the children for their games, sitting with the family around the dinner table, I stayed with them until the last light went out. With them, I enjoyed the first taste of grapes and the fruit from their trees. I experienced their fear every time soldiers approached their door, and I breathed their sigh of relief when the soldiers moved on. I bestowed names and characteristics on each member of that family: what they liked or hated, the innocent jokes they told at breakfast, what they wore on holidays, the color of the curtains in the sitting room, and what the husband said to his wife, both what she believed and what she discounted as lies.

That lasted until October arrived and wrote a new book of Exodus for us, though its story of liberation is not yet complete and continues to be written until this very day. October of 1995 was the date scheduled for handing Nablus over to the Palestinians. But that transfer would be preceded by a second transfer of a different kind: a long convoy of iron beasts, their bellies filled with betrayed, forgotten souls who had no voice to speak their pains. Those prisoners searched their suitcases and their walls for gods to cling to when they went forth into a new wilderness. The failure of the old story terrified them. The lies they used to believe had vanished, leaving them trembling and afraid. The iron bustas roared and bellowed, and with their approach, fear rose until it became a faith. The gods of the long journey descended to comfort the praying, trusting souls. Carrying with them all they could, the prisoners cast a final glance upon walls they had previously renounced when they thought they'd be set free. They found their walls just the same as before, firm and secure: walls that did not betray a promise nor turn their back upon anyone.

On the final day, I sat on my bed, leaning against my wall. One last time I looked at the small family that had begun going about its daily routine, caring nothing for what was about to happen to this person looking out at them. Just like every other day, they prepared the breakfast table. The children left for school. The mother emerged on her roof. My impending departure did not cause their hearts to skip a beat. It did not quicken their breaths. I didn't blame them, nor did I draw out my words of farewell. From my fixed vantage point, I watched what went on inside the prison, and I leaned harder against my wall. No speech passed between my wall and me that might disturb our solitude and our unity.

Around us, many souls were looking out the windows and casting a final look of reproach upon that imitation city with its fake memory. Fearful eyes that had not yet found a clear definition of what they feared, so they gave up the search. As they picked up those heavy souls, the iron bustas were transformed into a time machine—or so it appeared from the nervous and frightened faces of those leaving one geography for another. The force of the iron beasts drove home their exile.

Meanwhile, everything inside me was ready to depart. My destination had been set as Beersheba Prison. I remained there only for a few months, after which I was transferred to Nafha Prison in the Negev Desert. There, something entirely new began for me, with endings I never could have foreseen.

In Prison...

in prison...
you are a confession of everything inside you
some of the words you speak
say a little about you, though they might convey things
you do not believe
or you begin to believe when your years weigh heavy
    upon you
and your senses grow brittle
and the place and the faces and the music
of the names around you mix together
and the difference between night and day
and the wall's approach, and you do not know
if it has come to buttress something inside you
or it has come to kill you

in prison...
you are what people say about you
there's nothing about you that deserves to be told,
    except
what they all say about you in your absence
you are their mistakes if they get it wrong

and when they understand
there is nowhere for you when all their ideas break apart
nor when they cohere
the place is filled with their tumult, no voice rises
above the noise
and you have no voice

in prison...
you bid farewell to mornings that come to greet a face
but not yours
and when morning appears, the pillar of light means
    nothing to you
except the disappearance of your shadow
and the burning of bodies before you and more that
    burn
after you
then evening comes
a moment of a longer shadow and the final hour
of the sun
the slow advance of darkness and the end of
a day that has weighed you down

in prison...
nothing testifies to your presence
you are not here
you are far from there
a there where nothing still recalls your little details
or misses you
you have no marks to communicate
when did you arrive?

how long will you stay?
is this line drawn by your hand and which of the
     concerns
condemns you?
is this really you? is there anything inside you
that still resembles you?

in prison . . .
ghosts of those you once loved and have hung as photos
upon your walls
have faces that do not grow old like yours
others have departed and you have hidden them far from
     your pain
so they will not disturb
the faces of those who remain
or weigh heavily upon your memory if you forget
and other half faces, which you have given
features and names and desires close to your hunger
who leap from their bed and come
quickly
to toy with your sleep

in prison . . .
your mistakes and sins come together, all those you have
     deferred
to the vastness of time and a multiplicity of intentions
the first woman you betrayed
your certainty about future days
your forgetting of your Lord
or your recalling Him

your despair of love
your submission to servitude
a homeland that makes few demands, whether you dwell
     in it or it in you
and mistakes you hold close
a small amount of all that you deferred comforts you
and justifies your cry for God's forgiveness

in prison...
you come to know what was unknown
your conversation after an hour, the amount of salt in
your coming dinner, the women who visit you at the
     start of
each night
your share of the sun
your mood before coffee and what it might become
afterward
the faces of your visitors, the smell
of your waiting
on which side you will sleep tonight and every night
the amount of air in your lungs
the taste of the morning after the first cigarette and the
     colors
of your mirror's annoyance when you start each day
by looking at your own face

in prison...
your hands are suspended, one for you and another that
     writes
your inability

to hang your waiting upon the first gibbet
to console your mother in your absence
or to forget her
to stop the hands of time from
speeding up
to destroy your wall, or to allow it to build you or
destroy you
to forget a woman you loved
who broke your heart
to remember the face of your father and to forgive his
    death
and your inability to reclaim a hand that once was
your hand

in prison ...
you are all you need when you abide
in yourself
when you accept that you know that you
do not know, and that tomorrow will not take vengeance
    upon your today
and that your horses await you if only
you look for them soon
and you stop fleeing from yourself and from your wall
you are all you need
so stop
these are your hours, this is your heartbeat, this
    existence if
you believe it
is entirely yours

in prison...
you can be what you want
the last of the false prophets
the first man to believe the Messiah and walk to him
    across the water
Aladdin or his lamp: whichever you prefer
a butterfly not long to live
Scarlett's lover from *Gone with the Wind*
or Scarlett herself
an Andalusian flamenco dancer
an Arabian horse in a distant land
a supernova that tarries before it dies
a balcony looking out upon the moon or upon a woman
even more lovely and distant
in prison, you can be everything you want
without any chains to shackle you

in prison...
you are your liberation from everything that will come
    and then nothing
comes
and all that is coming is you
you are the place, you are the time
you alone
in prison you
possess everything and nothing
is yours

My Lord

I was born to parents who were believers. They believed in a simple Lord, with various names and descriptions, who sent His messages and made simple, uncomplicated demands. My parents railed at Him when we went to bed hungry, but they quickly reconciled with Him once reassured that we were sleeping soundly. They prayed, fasted, and performed as many other obligations as they could. My father sometimes embellished the words of his Lord, ignoring all my attempts to correct him. My parents did not impose their faith upon their children. Nothing came fast for them except love for their little ones.

My mother had a relationship with her Lord that was equal parts strange and hilarious. On the one hand, there was a kind of flirtation that she carried on throughout the day. Although my mother's love vocabulary contained only a limited number of words, they were enough for her and her Lord. But when she had something to complain about, she launched into one of her extended tirades, using words and phrases that could not have been deemed quite pious, had we examined them closely. My mother possessed any number of these expressions, and my brothers and sisters and I used to provoke her merely for the sake of listening to the way she blamed her Lord and criticized the events and individuals He allowed into her life. Gathered around her and listening in, we'd nearly die from laughter.

Growing up, my image of the Lord was the one drawn by my parents. The neighborhood children contributed other elements inherited from their parents. As the circle of my movements and acquaintances widened beyond the camp, I added yet more features. In this way, and after I had removed anything that contradicted the ambitions, hopes, and desires of a youth who embraced his curiosity and rejected all forms of constraint, I ended up with an amalgamated image of a Lord who suited me as closely as He resembled me.

I based my religious observances upon imitating my parents, though I grew bored by the repetition. I would pray for a week or two and then stop for several months. From the age of eight, however, I began the devotion of fasting for Ramadan, which I maintained unless some interruption was warranted. As my age increased, my prayers decreased. In a kind of adolescent compromise, I lived in perfect harmony with my Lord. He forgave all my small sins—or so I imagined Him doing. As I grew older and my sins grew larger, so did my Lord's forgiveness, and within that comfortable balance, I lived a happy adolescence.

That happy state lasted until I reached the age of fifteen, when one of the women in the camp made a project of winning my affections. Sometimes with words and sometimes with actions, she flirted with me. She kept flirting until she became tired of waiting for a man who was as slow to comprehend as he was to grow up. She decided to move things along and found the most inventive way of achieving her objective. That encounter with her overwhelmed my senses and left my body numb. I felt angry, I felt exultant. Afraid of the new world I had discovered, I fled. Just a few days later, I came back. My senses were more overwhelmed, my body more numbed. I became seriously angry, then even more jubilant. I feared what more there was to discover, and I fled a second time, faster than before.

When my stumbles lost their simplicity, my adolescence became more difficult. My Lord needed to grow even larger, with a forgiveness that expanded to meet all the new discoveries in my life. This new stage made the following eight years an experiment in living, and I was unprepared to understand all the new worlds that I explored. But those eight years also equipped me for the longer project of life yet to come. My Lord continued to watch over my steps, both in my adolescence and the subsequent years of my rebellious young adulthood, during the Intifada of the Stones, and on my path to prison.

Given an intifada suffused with enough death and danger for an entire generation, and given my adventures of the erotic kind—an intifada that stripped my body naked and destroyed its peace by making it grow up too fast—I needed a Lord who was closer, more merciful, and more forgiving. A Lord who comes down from His heaven to dwell in cramped neighborhoods filled with soldiers, the smell of gunpowder, and souls seeking some escape from pursuit. A Lord who stands between us and the bullets that ripped through our bodies. A Lord who would not receive our dead but return them to rejoin the fight alongside us. A Lord who stands at the door to knock, and when we are too proud to answer, knocks a second time, and a third, until we open the door of our heart. A Lord who waits for my prayer, even if I'm slow to cry out to Him, and who responds even if I stop praying. A Lord who knows all my needs and even those I've forgotten. A Lord like the Lord of my mother and my father, who does not become angry if I add to His alphabet or blame Him in my delusion and my weakness.

Fear was not what led me to seek a Lord who would come closer to me. Instead, it was my need for a companion from beyond this world, someone who did not acknowledge its natural laws and its various customs, traditions, and cultures. A capacious presence who would abide by my mistakes without pronouncing hasty judgments upon me or divulging my secrets to anyone. I would not be ashamed to practice my most shameful habits in His presence. With Him, I would drop all my masks, all my false words. A divine companion, one whose laws and geography would not stunt my emotions or limit my marvelous adventures. One who would not stone me, whip me, threaten me, or provoke fears I couldn't endure. I needed a Lord who would stand beside me if all those closest to me abandoned me. A Lord who would not be afraid to enter confined places if I were unable to liberate myself and soar above them. A Lord who would stroke my chest when I felt myself choking, who would ease the pain of my heart whenever it was breaking.

In this way, my Lord became just as I wished Him to be. I fled to Him when the alleys narrowed and the soldiers cut off my escape. I fled to Him between one bullet and the next. I fled to Him after paying my respects to the last martyr. I fled to Him when I was detained and when I confessed, down in the vault and above ground. I fled to Him every time my world contracted and all paths were lost. I made Him dwell beside me, very close, for I only dwelt upon the walls. My Lord occupied a broad expanse in the mural I made, fighting and competing for every inch of it. He never tired of dwelling beside me, nor did He despair if I grew stubborn and quarreled.

The three of us remained like that: me, my Lord, and a most confining space, existing together upon a single wall. From that position of reconciled stability, I created some worlds and destroyed others. I altered the positions of stars and planets. I lengthened and then shortened the passage of seasons. Everyone has a Lord they pray to and praise, whose face they rise to receive first thing in the morning. I had a Lord I loved and who loved me. I received His face at any hour I wished, even when I slept through the morning prayer: a Lord of faith and a Lord of belief; a Lord of mistakes and a Lord of good intentions; a Lord of the rich and the poor and those in between; a Lord of place and time, what came before them and what will come after; a Lord of the stones and the bullets; a Lord of the soldiers and a Lord of those they pursued; a Lord of wars and defeats and victories; a Lord of fathers and mothers, a Lord of little children; a Lord of lovers when they remained faithful and even when they didn't.

Me, my Lord, and a most confining space: the three of us continued our dialogues upon the surface of the wall. While we were in the belly of an iron beast that carried us deeper into the Palestinian desert of Negev, that wall was waiting for us. In a few hours, we would be reunited in Nafha Prison. Throughout the journey, our lungs were filled with dry air, and I was enveloped by an intense feeling that I was leaving for good. The closer we came to our destination, the shallower and faster came my breaths. I was unable to explain that feeling, so I waited for some change in my condition. But it remained just as it was, and the iron walls of the busta closed in tighter. Then the vehicle stopped at the prison gate, and every sound died away.

Farewells

Shortly before dawn, Buthaynu saluted
my camel and set off;
Return the greeting! How can you not
return the greeting, O my camel?

—KUTHAYYIR (D. 723)

When reading our pre-Islamic poetry, I have always marveled at its rich vocabulary for describing a desert landscape whose native alphabet was limited to sand, thistles, the burning sun, and a scarcity of water. The depth of emotion and the refined sensibility of this poetry is astonishing. How could that be, given the severity of nomadic life and the harsh nature of the tribe, which would avenge a slain beast by killing a thousand men? I marveled at its faith and the gods it fashioned when the tribe prospered, only to eat those same gods when the hunt or the harvest failed. I marveled at its ability to invent a hundred or more synonyms for every noun. Pre-Islamic Arabs possessed a remarkable genius for poetry. We have wronged it, in our ignorance, by calling that poetry jahili, meaning "ignorant," transferring the term previously applied to the pre-Islamic era.

How could the desert possibly imbue a rough Bedouin with the clarity of water and the softness of grass? How did that Bedouin arrive at all his gods when there was nothing to see around him besides repression, coercion, and a world that abounded only in hunger and thirst? Was there something in the horizontality of the desert that inspired our Bedouin forebears with a verticality that made him soar into the sky and fill that emptiness? Was there something in his nomadic solitude that made him personify his material surroundings and give voice to the night, the day, and the heavenly bodies? That made him address his mount and hear its reply? Along with a tradition of burying infant daughters, the Bedouin also buried his fears and anxieties. He buried poverty and class distinctions. He went on burying until his desert was transformed into a mass grave that contained everything that troubled his existence. Upon the traces of those graves, he composed his literature and his poetry, writing things about his women that no one else has ever managed to say, either before or since.

In November 1996, I, too, was in the desert. All was silent as the busta filled with prisoners stopped in front of Nafha Prison. Its great gate opened, and long hours of waiting settled upon us. After a humiliating inspection, we gathered in the visitation hall, waiting to be divided into its various blocks and rooms. The prison had four blocks, where nearly four hundred prisoners hung from the walls, enclosed within rooms and courtyards so narrow that the sun grew tired of being confined within them and moved quickly on. Small desert courtyards, surrounded by a prison, which itself was encircled by unending desert. The sky above was empty apart from a few wretched birds, the sound of military planes training to fight us, and a fine dust that made breathing a painful task.

By evening's end, we were all in our rooms. Eight souls huddled together to ward off the winter chill. After some prolonged introductions, I jumped onto my upper bunk. A window looked out over a back courtyard that contained nothing but sand and dust, barbed wire, and the barking of guard dogs.

My wall was there, waiting for me to arrange my things so we could be alone again and prepare for our first morning. But first, we had to explain the sense of suffocation that came over me during the journey in the busta. I looked at myself. I looked at my wall. Then I looked for my Lord in all His usual places, and I did not find Him. His disappearance did not make me anxious. I searched again, more carefully this time. I found nothing but His absence upon the wall. I looked at the other souls around me, who had also been abandoned by the imitation cities, the villages, and the camps. These souls had been buried here under the desert sands, far enough away that their screams of pain would not disturb anyone's sleep. I returned to my wall. It had freed me from a Lord whom I did not blame for any of the remarkable things that had befallen us: this is where we part, you and I. The wall was filled with the sense of that leave-taking. I kept repeating my thought: this is where we part, you and I.

In the seven years that followed, I would do without a Lord who had accompanied so much of my life. I abandoned my daily prayers and devotions. I fell upon the wall that was my stable point of reference, and I clung to it like never before. Seven full years in which I would flee my Lord and His mercy, His consolation, His threats, His approach, and His withdrawing. I would flee His books, His prophets, and

His gardens filled with women and silk robes. I would flee His iron-melting fire. I ignored my Lord's repeated knocking at my locked door and returned to the jahili desert with its multitude of gods. I let go of all my life that came before or after, and I held fast to my wall and all the life it contained: I am my wall, and my wall is me. I offer my years to it as a sacrifice, and it neither tires of me nor abandons me.

My scribbling expanded across the wall, especially after my rejection of any divine presence there. I needed that space amid the crowded confinement that closed in upon me each day. Before long, I had habituated my breathing to the dust that choked the air. I learned how to sleep despite the incessant barking of dogs. My steps no longer felt constrained by the throngs of feet in the narrow courtyard during our hours in the sun. Without protesting too much, I learned to accept the reality that the desert always gets the final word.

Meanwhile, my wall existed above every physical phenomenon. Nothing about it was affected by variations in our environment. It cared nothing about my parting from my Lord so long as I continued clinging to it. My wall may even have preferred my return to that jahili state of ignorance, given its own paganism and a small Kaaba whose cramped walls contained all the gods, with no strife between them, no driving away, nor rejection, nor killing on the basis of identity. The wall was pleased for me to live like my ancestors, the jahili Arabs in their desert. I searched for life inside myself after every possibility for life in the desert proved in vain. Out of the sand I fashioned gods that I killed if my desert ran out of other blood for me to shed. I slept with all the women of the tribe and with the women of the neighboring tribes. Upon the sinuous twisting of the wall, I wrote a thousand poems in symmetrical lines. I rejected all the prophets, for no religion tempted me apart from the religion of my tribe. Instead of the Kaaba, I circumambulated around my wall. I hung upon it my poetic creations of love and war.

More than a year went by in Nafha Prison. My existence was my wall and me, with no third beside. Souls there lived each day as though it were their last. They recalled their former life when seeing it in the eyes of visitors, but forgot it again when they returned to their sand and dust. They prayed and fasted and slept. They grew old and wept for a homeland that had abandoned them. My wall and I survived sandstorms and the desert cold, which showed no mercy to our brittle bones. We held fast to our old legends and our lies about the land. In doing so, we were like other souls who also found a certain stability in the stories they told themselves.

I kept living my days and nights and thought my routine would continue forever, without any new blows of fate to disrupt my balance. Then March arrived with a visit from my mother. Sitting across from her, I noticed nothing about her face looked right. She remained silent. So did the relatives who were present, watching her. I noticed my father's absence and asked my mother about him. She made no reply. Then she began crying. My father was gone.

I fell out of my chair. When I awoke on my bed that evening, I saw my fingers were bloodied from striking the iron grate that had separated a mother weeping for her beloved husband and my own weeping for a father. My head fell back against the wall. Exhuming my father from his grave, I sat him on the bed in front of me and began expressing my regrets.

"I'm sorry, Father, for your death and for your life. For your land, and what you forgot about working the soil. For the expulsion from your house, for exile in the camp, and for your poverty, your ignorance, and all the emotions you repressed. I'm sorry, Father, for every time I didn't kiss your face, for every time I deepened your sense of impotence, every time I blamed you when it wasn't your fault, every time I was ashamed of your empty hands and your wobbling cart, and every time I called you father without calling you lord. I'm sorry for every conversation between us that was cut short, and every time I interrupted your time alone with Mother, whether I meant to or not. I'm sorry, Father, that you ignored me during our visits, and for everything you wanted to say but didn't. I'm sorry for being surprised at your death, and for being absent from your washing, your burial, and all the good things that people said about you. I'm sorry for weeping, and that I never wept for you before. For my paganism, and for not possessing a single coin to place upon your eyes to speed the final crossing."

I apologized to my father for many other things besides. But I also recalled every beautiful moment we spent together. My father had placed all his dreams upon my shoulders, and I hung them upon the wall. Then this father died, and I can still see the yearning that transformed his face every time we visited his abandoned, plundered village. My father died without bidding me farewell, and how badly I needed to say goodbye! My father died, still blaming and censuring me, before I could explain my absence or make him understand the reasons for what I did. My mother said he went to sleep every night crying, far from everyone's eyes, but he never once cried in my presence. Now I cried for him like I never wept for anyone before. I'm still crying for him, in case he will look kindly upon me and forgive me. I speak all the words of love I know. I tell him our old stories and the legend of the land, and that we have planted enough trees to shade and feed everyone who fights, trees that will rise and fight in our place if we die. I tell him about his village. Its thistles have grown taller than me, it still has figs and almonds, and the big carob tree is still standing where it used to provide us shade each time we stole back there. I tell him how my mother is doing after his departure, and that she keeps getting more and more beautiful with each passing year, and that she refuses to die because I would call it a betrayal if she did.

When you are stricken by the death of someone dear, what you need is a solitary corner you can retreat to, either to heal in peace or else die in silence. Such a place is the last thing to be found in a narrow, crowded room. I was forced to endure all those souls who took it as their religious and humanitarian duty to impose themselves upon my grief. They swarmed around me with bizarre questions about my father. They whispered in my ear all the verses from the Qur'an about patience, together with the Prophet's sayings about forgiveness and the certainties of death.

I waited for the questioners to leave me alone so I could return to my wall. From inside my sadness, I looked upon an existence bereft of my father, and I pondered what that existence would be: Would I curse it, or would I reconcile with it and come to embrace it? My wall had plenty of room now that my Lord had departed from it, so I brought another lord who had died only a few days before, and I buried him upon my wall. I began reciting over my father the verses he had relied upon, and which still meant something to me. I prayed for him to have another life, an existence that knew neither poverty nor absence. I might even pray for him to have another woman as beautiful as my mother, if that were possible, and if my mother would allow it.

During that year and more in Nafha Prison, I first separated from one Lord who did not die. But then another lord died, and his death still hurts with a pain that does not ease, shows no mercy, and never dies.

The Al-Aqsa Intifada, 2000–2005

The years 1993 through 2000 were punctuated by attempts on the part of Palestinians and Israelis to negotiate. Even though Israel stubbornly refused to carry out its obligations according to the agreements it had signed, that didn't prevent the souls in prison from achieving a certain stability. There was measurable progress in their living conditions that went beyond anything seen throughout the previous decades. Prison administrators eased their iron grip, softening regulations and responding more positively to the prisoners' demands. These changes could not compensate in any significant way for the painful disappointment that came from being abandoned, but the souls took advantage of the new atmosphere to win yet more concessions that improved their daily life.

Our sole consolation was that we would be the last generation of Palestinians to hang upon the walls, hidden away in the prisons of the Occupation. We wanted to believe that the gates of the prison had closed for good, and that no new souls would knock on the door and send us back to the beginning. We wanted a fast, peaceful death, with no labored breaths to trouble the world that we relinquished when it turned its back on us. We ate more, we slept longer, we grew old.

Our conviction provided a sense of accomplishment at a time when we came to realize that everything the Palestinians achieved had vanished into nothing. The new story being told, with all the lies it contained, had stalled. Sentenced to death on the day it was born, all attempts to revive it failed. Palestinians struggled with all their might and offered more concessions than they had the capacity to endure. The occupied lands became all the more submissive and suffered even more. Palestinians raised their voice in protest by blowing up their bodies in the face of the Occupation. Israelis raised their voice in protest by slaughtering people praying in mosque courtyards. Other forms of protest took various shapes and forms on both sides.

Well along our own way to death, we anxious souls in prison watched Palestinian society being transformed. Upon my wall, I, too, tried to read the events abstractly, uninfluenced by my anger, my frustration, and my accusations. The picture had become much more complicated due to the partial implementation of so-called agreements that disfigured the historical and geographical contours of the land. With no prior preparation, the Palestinians rapidly transitioned from a revolutionary posture to a civilian one. They buried the old legend under the new thing they had constructed. They abandoned the economy of resistance and built a market economy that made them hostages to the economy of the Occupying State.

Although the Occupation continued shirking its obligations under the agreements, the Palestinians could muster no appropriate response, apart from some brief squalls that quickly blew over without altering the course of events. The prisoners followed those developments with alarm, and I took part in our numerous discussions to analyze the political situation. I expressed my fear that a new Palestinian generation, which I dubbed the Oslo Generation, had been pulled away from the old legend and offered a new one that would divert the course of its natural development. Instead of resistance to an occupation that continued to devour its land, it would accept invitations to a life filled with new discourses.

The new story was characterized by words of living and of life. Death remained present but was relegated to the wide margins of the page. It was the exact opposite of our old story, which was filled with narratives of death and pushed celebrations of life to the periphery. At the same time, this new story weakened the shared national identity. Local, familial, and other identities were reinforced, as were the differences in the social and economic structure between the West Bank and the Gaza Strip. The differences between those two halves of the story gestated through many years of occupation. Unable to bridge their disparate identities, they splintered further under the pressure of the new story.

The year 2000 saw a final attempt to revive the peace process. It quickly died, and with it, the new story died entirely. Its authors lost the ability to make Palestinians believe their lies about life, about reconciling time and place, and about an enemy's retreat. The discourse of the Palestinian leaders contained only one-fifth of a story, and it did not approach the fullness of the old legend: just one-fifth of the land, one-fifth of the history, one-fifth of the time and place. They relinquished its other four-fifths, which combined with the sea, shore, and sky to form the full legend. After grasping just a part of the story, the Palestinians found themselves falling into a black hole of history.

In September of that year, all the elements of an explosion were ready. The words of the new story had splintered in the faces of its supporters. Death emerged from its margins and once again occupied the center of the page. After Ariel Sharon's painful incursion, the squares around Al-Aqsa Mosque rose up against him, professed the old stories, and were washed with the blood of praying men.

Watching from deep inside my wall, the scene surprised me. The occupied streets quickly turned red as they cast off seven lean years filled with lying promises, distorted geographies, and grand solutions that had yet to utter a single word. I saw a generation of heretics who denied all that they had been made to believe. I saw them yearning for the old revolutions. I saw them fighting and dying, winning and plundering. I saw this generation in their black hole, hanging between two stories and no longer distinguishing between them. A chaotic fever struck the deepest core of their emotions. They fought without knowing the geography they were fighting for. They fought without knowing the history they were fighting for, now that all horizons and timelines had disappeared. Enraged, the Palestinians fought their wrath and those who incensed them. They fought their confusion and the loss of every clear text. They fought placelessness and timelessness. They cared nothing for the hour of their death or in what land they died. They dug deep in their memory to discover the old songs about death. Then they wrote new songs and went on dying. The jahili Arabs may have eaten their gods, but the Palestinians ate their own flesh. They went on eating till they could eat no more.

The Oslo Generation became the Second Intifada Generation, and they fought as Palestinians had never fought before. They let go of all the discourses and held fast to their original holy ground, where they died and from where they were resurrected to heaven. Meanwhile, the elite fled to their books and their caves. They abandoned an entire generation with no compass to guide it. This generation fought alone, with no angel to protect them and no divine care to rescue them from a sky filled with iron ghosts that shredded their limbs. They fought like prophets and sinned as though each day were their last. They sought refuge in the imitation cities, only for fearful doors to be slammed in their faces, having forgotten the discourse of popular resistance. So the Oslo Generation did their work at a distance from their audience in the cities, villages, and camps. They fought in anger, in pain, and to seek revenge, without caring where that anger, pain, and vengeance would take them. This intifada generation just kept on fighting.

We watched their war, hanging from our wall. Nothing we knew came even close to what we were seeing. We saw the Occupying State seized with fear, their normal life routines paralyzed. They tried every form of killing, every variety of individual and collective terrorism, but nothing worked. They warred against combatants and noncombatants alike. They warred against streets and houses. They warred against fields and livelihoods. They warred against women, old men, and children. Bullets pierced Muhammad al-Dura after passing through a father who tried in vain to shield his son with his own body. There was more killing, much more and even uglier, but it did not keep a generation from deciding to die.

On the other side of the planet, some Salafi Islamists were building themselves a new foundation called al-Qaeda. They soared through the sky aboard the very modernity they denounced as infidel. Twin towers were destroyed, and the world declared its war. Armies were mobilized, and the universe filled with speeches of vengeance and reprisal. Everyone oppressed by hunger, poverty, religion, creed, frustration, or marginalization flocked to an Islamist banner that proclaimed a message as marginal as itself. They all began fighting and dying in the name of a religion of peace that rarely sanctioned war or granted permission to kill.

After 9/11, the situation in the Palestinian square became more complex. The local killing machines were no longer enough to suppress the Second Intifada Generation. They were joined by machines even more deadly and destructive, powered by the discourses of vengeance. All sides became more extreme, and the elite once again disappeared from the scene. All attempts at pacification and cease-fires failed. The Palestinians fought on, unchecked by globalized plots against their ability to die. They made their enemy suffer as much as they were able. The Occupying State grew tired of killing. It destroyed the squares and streets of the imitation cities. It besieged Yasser Arafat, the Chief Storyteller, in his neighborhood. It sought to kill or detain every fighter. It resumed its former occupation. The people kept vigil in their homes with their fear. All voices subsided, save a solitary voice that continued crying out against a siege from which no one saved him. The Occupation increased its blockade of the Chief Storyteller, tightening the noose around his neck, and still he did not stop crying out his imprecations. The occupiers closed in. They despaired of waiting for death to silence his voice, so they killed him.

We had found comfort in believing that we were the last to be hung upon the walls in a long exile. But oh, how naive we were!

Pain

*People can endure every kind of pain except
the pain they don't understand.*

—NIETZSCHE

If only we were the last to be hung upon the walls! Having surrendered to a fate created by hesitant, uncertain hands, we sank into a deep sleep. We began to pray for the inevitable extinction of our sorrows, as though to hasten our own end.

The Al-Aqsa Intifada changed all that. I was transferred again, leaving the desert and returning to Ashkelon Prison. There, we found crowds of new souls who had begun their own journey to find a place upon our walls. The detentions increased. The interrogation blocks were crammed with thousands of prisoners pouring in. There weren't enough walls to hang them on. Old walls were reinaugurated to absorb the unending waves of souls who had come to hang upon a wall for the first time.

For various reasons, both geographic and demographic, I and a number of other old souls were transferred back to Nafha Prison and the desert. We were chosen to prepare those cellblocks and to welcome the newcomers in a way that might ease their first days upon the wall. After supplying the empty rooms with everything necessary, we sat and waited for the first prisoners to arrive. This task meant I had to emerge from my deep slumber upon my wall. I had to abandon my isolation, my solitude, and the monotony of my daily routine. I emerged without a Lord to worship or a father to take my Lord's place. All I had was a mother, whose visits the Occupying State had decided to forbid. I also possessed a strength sufficient to sustain my hanging. Filled with contentment and acceptance, I was ready to join the new souls, some of whom were crushed by the pain of fresh wounds.

Which pain cuts deeper: a new pain or one that has grown old and aches inside with a familiar echo? What hurts more: all that we've let go, or that to which we still hold fast? Our presence in this actual life, or our absence from some other possible life? Does it sting more to part from our lovers, or to hear the names and descriptions of those who have taken our place? How far do the borders of our pain extend, and what lies beyond? Can a wound dwell in just one part of us, ignored by all the other parts? What happens when one wound covers up another? Does the first one heal, or is it just buried deeper?

When we sustain a wound in body or spirit, the first thing we become aware of is the pain, a fault line running through our constitution that intrudes upon our consciousness and impedes our control over the various functions of our body. The resistance we feel from our body alarms us as the pain exercises a will of its own. It defiantly rises up whenever it wishes, and it tumbles down after changing its mind. It sleeps on any side it wants while exiling us to the margins of sleep. It either recovers in its own way, or it dies after becoming bored of our tedious company.

Various pains are tolerable, but what we cannot endure is the suffering they produce. Pain is limited to some defect in our body, but our consciousness is overwhelmed by suffering when we expect our pains to end. That expectation transforms the pain into a torment. We cannot bear it, and we are incapable of finding a cure, because no medicine can reduce the expectation we feel. Amid that suffering, all forms of life break down, and everything within us comes to a halt. Through that expectation of relief, suffering slips into our consciousness and makes the torment of our wounds permanent. There is no longer any possible alternative. It is only when we release our expectations and instead embrace our pains, clinging to them fiercely, that we become able to expel the torment and rescue our consciousness from the suffering that has taken over.

In prison, suffering is able to bind every element within you. It divides you from yourself, from your ego, and it is as though you have no self. It can mount you, bleeding, upon a cross, though no one sanctifies your flowing blood. It is able to paralyze every changing thing within you. Suffering arrives to your bed before you. It wakes up an hour before you do. It washes your face without any water. It makes your breakfast and fills up your cup of tea—or coffee, if that's what you drink. It gets to the visitation room ahead of you and reveals all your lies to your mother. In prison, suffering distorts everything you do.

When I was first hanging upon the ghostly wall inside the interrogation block, I suffered an unbearable torment. One of

the ways the interrogators found to break us was the sound
of classical music that penetrated our ears until it blurred the
bodies of everyone hanging there beside me. We had no way
to rescue our ears from the noise of musical phrases that were
so complicated for an Eastern disposition saturated by the
quarter tones of our musical maqams. Despite my ignorance
of its strange systems and the ballroom dancing steps it was
composed for, I decided to enjoy the music. In one of those
masculine impulses that still surprises me, I would imagine
the most beautiful women and remove half the clothes that
concealed their secrets. We'd dance in a remote courtyard,
upon a distant planet, in a time not yet begun. With every
song, I chose a new partner, and none of them objected to
my boorish insistence upon selecting outfits for them, only
to strip them off later. Instead of waiting for the day's end to
bring relief, I embraced a music designed to break me.

For seventeen years, I experienced that kind of reconciliation with the pain of my wounds. Otherwise, I never would
have been able to survive my confinement. Things are what
we want them to be. "Make any decree you care to make, for
your decree applies only to this earthly life" (Qur'an, Taha
20.72). That's what the magicians said when they defied the
murderous Pharoah of Egypt, but I did not repeat their words
to my judge. Instead, I embraced my life sentence and ush-
ered it out of the occupier's courtroom. I carried its heavy
weight back to my cell in the isolation block. My life sentence
lacked the power to deprive me of my life, for I had already
bid it farewell upon the black wall of the interrogation vault. I
planted my life sentence upon my wall. I did not condemn it
or struggle against it. I made a home for it alongside my other

wounds. It was a kind of judgment upon my former life. The coming days mattered nothing to it, nor did it matter to those days. I saw it as a wound I bandaged without expecting it to be healed. I cursed it, but only with a good-natured bickering. Then we would make up, and it quickly forgave, like one always ready to reconcile.

The Turkish poet Nâzım Hikmet says, "You are able to spend twenty years in prison, or more, provided that the essence sleeping under your left breast does not blacken within you." Were it only a matter of the heart! Then we all could have endured our prison. Instead, it is a matter of pure consciousness, a matter of making the decision to define our surroundings not according to the meanings previously attached to them, but according to our own terms. We are able to endure any kind of pain if we decide to embrace, accept, and submit to its existence within us. If we stop expecting it to end, and banish from our minds a focus on how badly it hurts. It is not enough simply to be aware of our pains. We need to understand them, to define the types and depths of each. Every wound has a tale, and in order to understand it, we must come much closer and embrace it. In our wounds, we no longer see just our pains, but we are aware of the meanings that exist before and after the pain.

In prison, I saw souls who had spent two decades or more without clinging to their wall, not even for a single hour. They were blind to it and only perceived all the life beyond it. The wall did not leave any noticeable marks on their bodies beyond the wrinkles that lined their faces. Likewise, there were souls who spent two decades or more with us and were then set free, and their first speech shook off the dust of prison completely. I swear, it was as though they had not spent a single day hanging in their prison. I was sad for those blind souls, and I was angered by how they shook off the dust of this place. What tale will they tell? Their wounds have no tale to be told.

After I returned to the old blocks of the desert prison of Nafha in February 2002, it took only a few days for the prison's four blocks to be filled with new pains and fresh wounds. Other veteran souls and I had prepared the rooms with everything they needed. We prepared orientation programs, omitting any complicated details out of kindness to the new souls, wanting to allow them space to catch their breath after having been chased down and captured.

It was not possible for me to receive and welcome the new souls while I was in my old state of hanging. They needed a hanging that resembled them, and there was nothing about our hanging that resembled these new souls. Experiences cannot be inherited, and every soul must define the nature of its relationship with its wall through its own unique tale. I chose to accompany these souls on their journey from the very beginning. I had to support them, to help them, to answer questions that were impossible for them to resolve. I told them what I knew about the wall, though not my wall specifically.

These new souls leapt onto their walls from a land that was torn between two competing stories. They believed part of the first, and they also believed part of the second, such that both narratives intermingled within them. The generation of the First Intifada possessed a story of Palestinian nationalism.

Combining a few universal truths with various regional and local elements, the elites of that movement had written about the land as a cultural and political space that would unify all Palestinians. It was our story: we memorized all its details, and it harmonized with the goals of our struggle. At that time, the Islamist discourse was marginalized and did not form any meaningful challenge to the nationalist movement.

The generation of the Second Intifada, on the other hand, grew up at a time when Palestinian nationalism had splintered. The forces of the Islamist movement had appeared in the public square, and they fought until they won popular acknowledgment for their discourse and their story. As a result, its currents made inroads among the Palestinians, who fell into a black hole where two conflicting narratives strove against each other over the history and geography of a land that was only large enough for one story.

I observed the new souls from nearby: virginal souls whose bodies were caressed by the wall at times, only to be roughly groped at others. I saw the first fumbling attempts at becoming attached, and the painful falls when souls frequently tumbled off the wall. I only got involved in cases so extreme that I feared some soul would be overwhelmed by the terror of their fall. Even then, I kept my involvement to a minimum. Some of the other old souls went too far in pushing the new souls to hasten their attachment, wanting them to discover a sense of stability in the prison. The new souls resisted this pressure. They insisted on finding their own way. Many of them succeeded, though many others fell. They would get up, begin hanging again, and write upon their walls with their own unique alphabet. They wrote what they knew and had experienced. They wrote what had sent them astray and caused them to lose their story.

This new writing did not impress the veteran souls, who interfered in every possible way. A state of mutual antipathy arose that would last for many years to come. The new souls wrote in all languages, and reading what they had to say was never easy. They wrote with the same chaos they experienced in the black holes of their life, all the while deeming it orderly. Upon walls already filled with old souls, they searched for a space of their own. They crowded the wall's spaces and staked their claim to the little room that was left. They refused any attempt to marginalize them and sought an acknowledgment of all that they had narrated upon those old walls.

Keeping company with the new souls, I spoke about pain and suffering, hoping something I said might illuminate at least one dark corner of their new domain, or else spare them a long torment by helping them understand the nature of suffering. I spoke at length about holding fast and letting go. For many of them, I may as well have been speaking a foreign language. Others listened carefully, with deep interest, which made me believe that my words might do some good. I said much about the old story, and its form of hanging, and the clear pain it contained. I said many other things about the virginal nature of their hanging and the similar, yet different, pain that it contained. I saw I was wasting my breath for those who had just arrived. So I began organizing my papers, which had been scattered by their arrival, trying to restore my old routine. When I was secure once again upon my stable wall, the mutual antipathy between the old souls and the new was clear to see. It would become even more apparent in the years to come.

Take your wound to the edge of any sky you wish. Beat it against every inch of your body. You die if your wound remains conscious, so let it die instead! Or let it sleep. Don't disturb its slumber by expecting it to heal. Reject all its claims of pain and suffering, for just like dreams, things only come true if we believe them. Be deeper than your wound. Be bigger. Don't exist on its margin: let it exist as yours. Let your prior life grant you a thousand other lives, with similar opportunities for pain. We are not our pains. We are everything that existed before them and everything that will exist after them. Don't fall in love with your wound. Don't ever be seduced by the role of a victim. You are the master of your wounds. In prison, you are your prison. Part of your prison is you. If your father falls, catch him. If the one you love leaves you, do not despair, and do not believe she is gone if her love was sincere. If your mother comes to visit, do not stop yourself from collapsing before her: those are your pains. So come near to learn the enormity of your pain! Don't be afraid to come closer, for all pains are possible except those we don't understand.

Slowly, the months went by. Without any prior wish on my part, God reestablished Himself upon my wall. His appearance there was preceded by an old seduction that tempted my soul. I would take one step toward God only to take one step back. I kept hesitating until someone dear to me came back into my life, a niece I had carried upon my shoulders as a child, more than a lifetime ago. She pushed me to embrace my Lord anew. That was the beginning of a new journey during which I left the desert for grassy fields, abandoning my existence as an enlightened jahili Arab. During my next transfer, when I departed Nafha for Hadarim Prison, situated upon lands of the occupied village of Umm Khaled in the center of Palestine, I would go in the company of my Lord. Together, we began a new project of hanging that would surprise us both.

Hadarim Prison

An offensive article about prisoners published in one of the Israeli newspapers brought me into conflict with the warden of Nafha Prison. The warden rewarded my insolence by transferring me to Hadarim Prison, which was designated for agitating souls whose recalcitrance interfered with the interests of the Occupation. Within Hadarim Prison, Block No. 3 was given names such as "the Citadel" and "the Safe" due to its extreme security measures. Fitted with security cameras that recorded almost everything, down to the rise and fall of each breath taken there, all the rooms were supplied with listening devices to capture every word spoken between those walls.

The Citadel consisted of two floors divided into forty small rooms. Only a few kilometers away from the sea, the prison was surrounded by vast groves of citrus trees. Yet the souls there were unable to catch a glimpse of their green and blue surroundings because the block was too low to see over the prison walls. Each cell of nine square meters contained just three beds, a number that suited my solitary nature. Despite harsh conditions stemming from the violent tendencies of an arrogant prison administration, I preferred my life there for the long hours it granted me to be alone with my wall, a space that was waiting for me to organize its elements any way I liked.

Only thirty meters separated the Citadel from another block of the Hadarim Prison complex, called Hasharon, which was set aside for female Palestinian prisoners. The block was close enough to allow fragments of conversations to pass between us, when necessary—and close enough for us to hear the screams of the women every time they were beaten by the soldiers who guarded them. Those screams would rouse us into confrontations with the prison authorities that ended with us being subdued or else with some settlement that placed limits on the degree of mistreatment. Whenever the female prisoners resisted oppressive policies, it was our role to support and back up their demands, and they were often able to achieve a kind of stability in their living conditions.

The Occupation did not practice any discrimination on the basis of sex: its subjugation and violence fell upon men and women in equal measure at a time when Palestinian women continued to suffer from various forms of repression and pressure in their own society. Under a slogan of "equal in subjugation, equal in resistance," Palestinian women insisted upon their right to take part in the revolutionary struggle, even though doing so brought them into conflict with a conservative, patriarchal society that locked them out of sight, like someone trying to hide his own nakedness.

Taking advantage of the new, extrafamilial spaces that existed within the discourse of national resistance, Palestinian women began a project of self-liberation from the societal bonds that had held them down and marginalized their role. They solidified the enormous energies and abilities hidden within them. Their progress moved slowly at first, but they gradually developed their roles until, within the space of a few years, they became an active element in resistance activities, with some standing on the front lines and others in the middle ranks.

Before the 1948 Nakba, women had been forced to be content with secondhand accounts of events monopolized by men. Women listened to the stories of men, be they farmers, laborers, merchants, fighters, teachers, or even completely shiftless. They retold the victories of men, and sometimes they recounted the defeats, if men chose to share that news instead of hiding it under their tattered clothing. They told of the bountiful harvest of men when the crop was good, and of their poverty when their earth devoured the precious things they planted. They told of men's honesty and the things men believed. They told of men's fear, omitting that they were at the center of that fear. They told of the men's Nakba and how it impacted their land, their livelihood, and their heroism. They told of men's faithfulness to their Lord. They told of men's acquiescence to their losses, no matter how great. They told of men's belief in the promises of an exodus. They told of their tents, and the keys that men hung there for doors that had been shattered, never again to be opened.

In 1967, the Palestinians added a second Nakba to their first. Palestinian women refused to perform their old role of oral witness to the story of the men. Instead, they began fashioning their own story. They wrote their own war and their own death, if they were killed. They wrote their own anger, when their bodies and souls were violated. They wrote their own poverty and hunger. They wrote their lies, which matched the lies of the men. They wrote of their sons, both those who returned and those who were buried far away. They wrote about a lover they took, or several. They wrote on the walls in the camp, in the village, and in the imitation cities. They wrote of their own house and what had been destroyed. They wrote about their faithfulness, if they were faithful, and they said little about their betrayals, out of consideration for those whom they betrayed. They told of their journey and their fatigue. They wrote about their prison when they were hung from the walls.

Twenty years later, the First Intifada empowered Palestinian women even more. They took their place beside the men, often standing in front of them wherever the battle was drawn. They rebelled further against prevailing societal injustices, leaving homes that were no longer safe and smashing doors that were closed against them. But they could not prevent the violence and the killing of the Occupation. They fought, they were martyred, they were detained. In the Second Intifada of Al-Aqsa, Palestinian women did even more. Their monumental abilities and sacrifices astonished the people. They lined up first among those who blew up their own bodies in the face of ruthless oppression—and in its belly. They wrote their own legends, recounting long periods of hanging on the walls of the prisons. In the prison squares, they etched the most incredible portraits of endurance under the mistreatment of their jailers.

Since 1967, the Occupying State has detained 27,000 Palestinian women: full-grown women, young women, and minors; mothers and grandmothers; even unborn children. The prison cells witnessed the first cry of newborns who stretched the wombs of mothers shackled in iron chains heavy enough to strain the walls they hung from. The children remained in the cells where they were born, nursed for an entire year by their mothers, while other prisoners shared in the caretaking, the night vigils, and the anxiety. In this way, the other women shared in a motherhood that their bonds denied them. They wove clothing and made dolls. They carried the babies outside and exhausted themselves providing shade from the sun. They whispered all the bedtime stories they remembered into the babies' ears.

Then ends the year in which the imprisoned mother is allowed to embrace the child she bore. Soldier-guards approach, and the mother embraces her child, planting it upon her chest. The soldiers come closer still, and the mother's fingers press into the infant's body to keep it from falling into their hands. The soldiers stretch out their hands as the child begins to wail in reply to its mother's pinching and weeping. The mother begins crying even louder. The rest of the prisoners join in the caravan of tears. Nothing checks the soldiers. All the gods of mercy have deserted the space. The mother begs for another hour to hold her child, swearing by all she holds dear to surrender the baby at the end of one final hour. Nothing persuades the soldiers. The mother calls upon her Lord, or anything else the people have made her believe, but the soldiers have no Lord. Hands and fingers yield; screams die away. The infant stops crying, exhausted by its tears. The rest of the prisoners embrace a mother who gave up her son when her strength ran out. The soldiers have won.

* * *

In the Citadel I found what I was looking for. I found bigger spaces that suited my individualistic tendencies and my constant need for another hour alone. It helped that the other souls there were influenced by that place, which led them to adopt more individualistic activities, just the opposite of the crowded rooms in the rest of the prisons, where even your breathing becomes a communal act. Those activities strengthened the individualism of many souls inside the Citadel without diminishing their sense of community. In some souls, however, it reinforced introverted tendencies, and they began closing the doors of their rooms for all hours of the day.

My days quickly fell into a new rhythm, as did the hours I spent with my wall. In the large prison courtyard, we had more than enough time in the sun. The winter here had plenty of rain, which I had seen so little in the desert. Some of the windows provided narrow views onto patches of green, which reminded me of the cycle of the seasons, and that it was now spring. Something about the atmosphere of the rooms made it easier to read or sleep, if that's what a person wanted. The Citadel provided me with all I needed. My arrival there brought an end to ten years of hanging upon crowded walls, and I needed a quiet moment to catch my breath.

In May 2004, my hopes for lasting peace and quiet were crushed by the policies of the prison administration, which increased its ruthlessness and oppression. We despaired of any dialogue with it, so we decided to launch a hunger strike. We did that on our own, without support from any of the other prisons. In an attempt to break the strike, the prison administration transferred some of the prisoners, including me. I continued the hunger strike at Beersheba Prison, and I kept going until the souls in Hadarim Prison decided to end their strike following promises to improve their living conditions. I remained in Beersheba Prison until August, when the souls there launched their own hunger strike, which ended after eighteen days with no progress to speak of. A new conflict with the prison authorities resulted in my transfer back to Hadarim Prison at the start of 2005. I found that conditions in the Citadel had been improved a little, which made it easier for me to keep hanging there and facilitated my independent pursuits. But that situation did not last long. At the end of the year, I was transferred, for no apparent reason, back to Nafha Prison in the desert. From there I went to Beersheba Prison yet again, followed by another return to Hadarim Prison in 2006, where I have remained through the time of writing these lines.

I returned to Hadarim with my old plans and projects, hoping this time that I might achieve them without any unexpected surprises to delay or interrupt them. I also carried with me the tragedy of a division that increasingly tore the body of the Palestinian story. That division, between the nationalist and Islamist discourses, deepened the geographical and historical crisis that Palestinians faced. Both of the discourses wore a distorted geography as they wrote their parallel histories, which could never reunite as long as each side held fast to its own narrative.

2011: Was It Spring?

Palestinians had diverged: geographically, historically, temporally. In the occupied West Bank, they lived in complete isolation from the besieged Gaza Strip. That division quickly permeated the prisons, where the prisoner movement also splintered. Prisoners aligned with Fatah lived in specific blocks, which they shared with all but one of the rest of the Palestinian groups. Hamas prisoners lived apart, taking with them their songs and anthems, their Friday sermons, their story of heaven and a faithful Lord. They took their ancient history and faces that resembled ours, with the same wrinkles. They took their hour of exercise under a different sun, far from our fire. They chose a different qibla for their extended prayers, rejecting our idols.

The Citadel remained—and does to this day—the only section of the prison where all the Palestinian groups lived in harmony despite their differences. All varieties of the faith found shelter under its concrete ceiling. Another of the block's characteristics was that its walls forced the souls hanging there to adopt a stance, preventing any and all forms of neutrality. You either had to let go or hold fast, love or hate, hang or keep sliding down. This was in contrast to other walls that allowed souls to keep them at a distance and live as though there were no walls to hang upon. The Citadel imposed a certain clarity. It passed judgments and revealed its reactions at whatever time and in whatever way it wished. In the Citadel, the wall is a partner in all situations. It is a witness to feelings and emotions. It is a judge of every manner of action, and it passes judgment even if people stop acting. In the Citadel, a white wall gets dirty quickly if you neglect it. It responds without hesitation and fills your day with a depression you cannot bear. It expands when interminable conversations contract upon you. It narrows if you are overwhelmed by a need for solitude in which to review your soul's accounts.

The years succeeded each other quickly. My mother resumed her visits, rushing toward me and compensating for lost time with the new lies that I prepared for her with exquisite care. My hanging became an even stronger dependence. My inner music harmonized with the dance of the white wall. A few gray hairs announced that my forties were approaching: the black on my head was entering an autumn that would soon run its course and fall. My back started to hunch a little under the force of natural phenomena, such as hanging, sliding, and friction, and other, supernatural phenomena that piled up until they weighed it down: things like hunger and thirst; poverty and the temptations of radicalism; wars; the easy spread of death; refugees and beaches filled with drowned women and children; subhuman, nationalistic discourses; a planet on the verge of collapse; a human race convinced of its divinity till the very end. People abandoned their faith, and the Lord postponed His punishment until some unknown date. So people went on killing us all the more, and we grew tired from the long wait.

The years between 2006 and 2010 abounded in universal frustration, pierced by the global economic crisis in 2008, which intensified the pangs of poverty. Many states stood at the abyss; some tumbled into its depths. Among Arabs, popular fervor presaged imminent explosions. Middle-class youth and older generations alike adapted new discourses of stolen rights, nonexistent citizenship, and the invisible millions—ideas far removed from the paternalism of the ruling regimes and their rotten bureaucracies. Throughout Palestine, the assassination of President Yasser Arafat in 2004 had elevated an old political elite whose role had been marginalized by Arafat's halo. That elite advocated a new path that abandoned the choice of resistance. For them, the only option was negotiation and "peaceful resistance," a concept articulated sheepishly and neglected even in its mildest form. The Occupying State exploited the poverty of Palestinian discourse and action. Nothing checked their abuse, and they gave a free hand to their domination, their appropriation of land, new settlements, and an unending expansion of existing settlements at the expense of Palestinian lands. The Palestinian response was limited to a weekly calculation of the new settlements and discussions about continuing the negotiations, despite the fact that negotiation—even after so many attempts—had produced nothing other than a surge of killing and appropriation, not to mention a deepening of the divisions among Palestinians.

The Arab Spring, which began in Tunisia before turning other Arab capitals green, was a surprise. I saw the slogans of our old discourse transformed into a movement that filled the squares with fervent young Arabs. They cried out for freedom and the fall of moribund regimes that had arrested the arc of history among us by paralyzing every sense of progress, flourishing, and modernity. What I saw filled me with optimism. I was certain that Arab citizens would finally arrive at nationalism. By abandoning local concerns, they would restore the cause of Palestine to the top of the list of Arab priorities, on both the political and the popular level. I rejoiced in a generation that had brought an end to the long decades of indifference and resignation implied by the phrase "Leave it to God." This generation was writing a new prologue—a new Fatiha—for a political and social constitution that would supersede everything that had gone before. I rejoiced that women were taking their place in the ranks of the movement after emerging from under men's abaya and the umbrella of custom and tradition. I rejoiced that the youth were escaping old, faded, and dusty texts as they stepped forward to express a progressive discourse, articulated in a modern vocabulary. I rejoiced at the optimism pervading the Arab world after centuries of frustration had buried our reservoirs of creativity and excluded us from the swift procession of modernity until that concept disappeared entirely from our sight, our hearing, and our consciousness.

Green spread from the squares of the Arab capitals until it reached the squares of our prison courtyards. Everything happening throughout the Arab world was a good omen for the future. So, too, was news of an imminent prisoner exchange deal between Hamas and the Occupying State. Dreams multiplied, and freedom's horizon appeared just beyond our fingertips. Everything around me was in motion. So were all the souls, both old and new. Everyone was counting down their final hours on the wall. They saw the exchange deal as a chance for freedom from their hanging, despite knowing that the deal would be limited to only a few hundred prisoners. Everyone lived in a state of fear and anxiety that their hopes would be disappointed.

In Egypt, the "Mother of the World," Tahrir Square turned green. An old pharaoh fell who sought to immortalize himself, his descendants, and his retinue with pyramids built upon the pain and poverty of the Egyptians, upon their hopes and dreams, upon their voices and their strangulation. The sky turned green. The clouds were filled with glad tidings of change and the beginnings of a new covenant for Arab countries that wallowed in their antiquity. I became even more optimistic, for the lies we used to tell were now coming true, along with our prophecies about the collapse of regressive Arab regimes. The renaissance was late in coming, but it had finally arrived as our old slogans jumped right off the walls and occupied the squares of Arab cities. Our legend was not a fable. Here were its heroes, filling the squares, and no fear would restore their former apathy. Here they were, forging their destiny with their own hands, and transforming their dependence into intentions and actions.

In October 2011, news arrived that the prisoner exchange had been ratified between Hamas and the Occupying State. The souls all rushed to their rooms, and everyone pulled out their radios to confirm the truth of the report. Local radio stations announced their intention to broadcast lists of names of those being released. For the souls, four of the five bodily senses were suspended: hearing alone remained. They brought the radios closer to their ears. The romantic and patriotic songs that came next caused many to curse the broadcaster's relatives and the station owners. Advertisements for beauty treatments or for home goods played on repeat. More insults and curses and waiting. Paper, pens, and hands, ready to record names at a moment's notice. Faces disappeared from memory; only names remained. Everyone recalled their relatives and friends, ranking them in their hearts and their emotions. Each soul counted up how much they stood to lose if they were passed over. Old souls found themselves at a crossroads where their organizational affiliation would determine the course of their long hanging. New souls who had only spent a few years upon their walls were frightened by a further period of hanging if their names fell off the lists in favor of those who had spent decades upon their walls.

Out of the thousands of souls, old and new, any deal would take only a few hundred. I returned in my mind to the prisoner release after the Cairo Agreement in 1994. The current situation was exactly the same, but now I had my old resources and my wall. It saved me once before and could save me again. In a voice betraying not the least emotion, the announcer began reading the names of the prisoners to be released. The names clearly revealed the priorities of Hamas. It was Hamas prisoners first, no matter how long they had been there. A painful reality, but I could accept it. I understood that movement's motives.

Shouts and calls began ringing out from the other rooms, even as the names continued to be read. My certainty that my name was not on the list did not relieve the tension and anxiety that overwhelmed my hanging. I became afraid, and I clung harder. "I must not fall; there's nothing below," I kept repeating to myself, trying to believe it. Then the reading of names was over. All the invitations to the party had been distributed, and none arrived for me. The chosen names celebrated loudly before suddenly falling silent. We all entered a liminal space. The invitees muted their joy at being welcomed back to life. The rest denied their sorrow. Each side chose their words carefully. The invitees would not hurt those who were excluded, and those left out would not spoil the joy of those going to the party. One man checked the smile that bent the corner of his mouth until he found a secluded corner where he could set it free. Another forced a congratulatory smile and sought a dark corner where the ghosts haunting his face could come out of hiding.

I rejoined my wall. In a mute voice, I told myself: "You have let go of that world, so don't try to hold on to it. These are your pains, so endure them." I imagined my first wall, where I had bidden the world farewell. Silently, I began to speak again: "Mount your imaginary horses and the mythical creatures you've invented. Your father has departed, and your mother has grown used to the constant betrayal of an absent son. No one will cry for you: they're tired of tears and of your perpetual lies. So don't fall. There's no life in falling, and nothing lies beyond it. Leap from all the walls within you and fall onto your own wall. You haven't put your Lord to the test before by demanding your release, so don't start now. Your Lord is innocent of all your fates and your pains. There's nothing to do but relinquish the world. All the great men of the tribe have died. You're the only one left, so stand up tall. Your mother still sings about her handsome son and the women who sleep in his arms until the first light of morning. She promises at every visit that she will not die as long as you go on hanging here."

I continued my speech, all alone, while other souls, both old and new, began packing their pains into small suitcases provided by the Red Cross, which undertook the responsibility of carrying out the terms of the agreement. The departing souls also packed clothes, redolent of familiar odors they had grown accustomed to in their final hours in the shadow of the wall and upon their road leading them away. The final hours contained many conversations that everyone wished would end quickly, along with the muddle of emotions they brought, so that souls invited to celebrate their lives could finally begin to do so, and the wall-souls could return to their walls.

This was a pain I understood. I had faced it before, nearly twenty years ago, and I have carried it like someone who endures his burdens. But this time, the weight was greater. These were souls who had been my companions from the very first days of my time on the wall. I knew the names of their pains and what they called their deferred joys. This was my old story and the lying gods who, like me, believed their lies. I knew their favorite foods at breakfast. I knew how they drank their coffee. I knew what their imaginary lovers looked like. I knew what spring had been like for each soul, and the distant memories that autumn left behind on their faces. Something like a feeling of exile settled within me throughout the weeks of my winter. It was not exile from a place, but an exile from souls. Eventually, when I passed by some of the cells, I started hearing the voices of those who used to be inside. I'd have to quicken my steps to keep myself from stopping. I had to call upon all my faiths and all my certainties in order to keep my balance, to drive away my feeling of estrangement, and to find ways to communicate with the new souls. It all took more time and effort than the previous occasion, almost two decades before, but I succeeded, and I returned to my hanging with a newfound sense of balance.

The Arab countries continued on their path, with much bloodshed and more death. In that stuttering, stumbling spring, the people's revolutions were stolen. Military uniforms washed away the stain of their defeats and occupied the seat of judgment. They proclaimed fearsome enemies, half of them imaginary. They colluded with the enemies of the nation in conspiracies against Palestine. The Palestinian political elite doubled down on its sole path of negotiating with an oppressor that had been seduced by its old story about Greater Israel and abandoned every pretense of peace. The Palestinians maintained their divisions, unable to resist the methodical plans of the Occupying State. Dreams evaporated. The entire Arab world entered a vortex of violence and chaos that generated nothing.

I got used to the absence of the old souls who were set free from their bonds, and I searched for previously overlooked connections with the new souls. Meanwhile, although the prisons increased their attacks on the prisoners' limited freedoms and comforts, a state of torpor infected the divided ranks of the prisoners, like a kind of paralysis, rendering them incapable of resisting the oppression. I maintained my equanimity until the president of the Palestinian Authority, Mahmoud Abbas, decided to enter a new round of negotiations in 2013. That venture would cost me enormously by plunging me for a third time into a confrontation with my emotions, my stability, and my faith.

The Fourth and Final Group

Here's what happened in 2013.

Barack Obama stunned the world by being elected president of the United States in 2008. In striking contrast to his predecessor, he traveled to Egypt to give a speech about reconciliation with the Middle East. Following in the footsteps of previous American presidents, but with better intentions, Obama made a solution to the Palestinian conflict one of the primary goals of his presidency. Yet this Black president was surrounded by a White government deeply committed to supporting Israel and preserving its economic and military superiority over its Arab neighbors, which severely limited Obama's opportunities for success.

Obama's first term ended without any notable progress on this issue. Immediately after being reelected in November 2012, he began applying pressure to bring both sides back to the negotiating table. The pressure worked. For a period of nine months, the Israelis and the Palestinians engaged in negotiations, guided by a working paper drafted by an American team led by Secretary of State John Kerry. Preliminary understandings included a Palestinian pledge not to apply to join any international organization while negotiations were underway. In turn, Israel pledged to release any prisoners who had been detained before the Olso Accords of 1993. One hundred twenty old souls were all that remained of that cohort, and Israel would release them in four groups, with no more than two months separating one group from the next.

Scattered among all the prisons, including thirteen in Hadarim Prison, these souls had been hanging upon their walls between twenty and thirty years. The marks that scarred my body reminded me of the necessity of controlling my emotions and of not straying from the stability of my safe zone. Even so, the temptation was great. Invitations to a life beyond the wall filled the air. The new souls buried their own pains as they came to announce the good news and celebrate the end of our long tribulation. Their joy for us eclipsed the anxiety we felt after so many disappointments over the years.

"Here, Sisyphus, is one last mountain to climb, so drop the stone from your shoulders. Heave a sigh for the end of your eternal ascents. The ground before you has been made plain, so stretch out and be comfortable. You have reached the other side of the mountain, so outrun your shadow and leave your stone behind. Forgive what you have lost from the springtime of your life. Take your autumn and your winter; take all the possibilities of a future life. Consign your anxiety to the ghosts you've left behind. Preserve your decades of companionship here and all the vows of faithfulness you have sworn."

These words and many others ran through my mind. I believed none of them. A thousand barriers stood between me and my ability to believe, no matter what the souls around me kept saying. The end of my hanging seemed an unreasonable thing to believe, foolish and reckless. This was not the first time that I had stood on the shore's edge, hearing the call of the waves. Yet each time, I sank into the dry land, where no water moistened my disappointments or washed the long years of waiting from my mother's face. I turned into a block of stone, and the wall etched its years upon me.

August approached, the month scheduled for the release of the first group. The progress of the days nearly came to a halt, no matter how hard people pushed them forward. Cursed is the middle ground between life and death, between thirst and drinking, between freedom and liberation, between the lovers we have and our admiration for ones we don't, between the wall and the sky. Cursed is the ambiguity of the middle: our wound until it heals, our waiting until it ends, our life until it begins, our patience until it is exhausted, our imprisonment until manumission, our death until resurrection, and our Lord until we receive what He promised.

For many days, I oscillated between letting go and holding fast, with nothing to ease my uncertainty. This was a place I had explored more than once over the decades, and I knew all its dark corners. So why did these false invitations to life tempt me? How had I allowed a gap between me and my wall to slip into existence? My stone felt heavier, and the mountain appeared higher and closer, daunting me with the prospect of climbing it each day. The desire just to let go and give in stirred within me. What will remain of you, Sisyphus, if you drop your stone? How can you abandon a pessimism that has never let you down? Into what abyss will you fall if you let go of your wall?

The names in the first group were announced. Two tired old souls in my block packed their years into small suitcases. One of them was a dark-skinned Gazan, headed for the sea and a dim, besieged strip of land. The other was headed for the Messiah's blessed city of Bethlehem, which had not perceived the absence of its souls for a single day, nor mourned them by extinguishing even one candle on its annual Christmas tree. Everyone began cheering and kissing each other. Some final words were spoken, some final goodbyes and an embrace. The new souls began talking about the next group and how short the wait would be. Suddenly, the small gap that existed between me and my wall during the recent weeks vanished. So, too, did the false life that tempted me and upset my balance. I made my final goodbyes and ran back to the wall. My stone was in its usual place. Pick up your stone, Sisyphus, for nothing compares to the joy of arrival like the effort of the attempt. Each time is the last. Each mountain is your final ascent. Don't stop in the middle.

It was two months until the release of the second group of prisoners. I stopped expecting anything at all, and my days regained their accustomed hue. Seeking to ignore the commotion on all sides, I plunged into dozens of books, reading anything that was available. Once more I listened to romantic songs. They sang of joys unavailable to me, but I could relate in my own way to the pains they expressed. I tried to ignore the souls who were already bidding me farewell, even while I was still among them. They kept talking about an imminent parting, and how much we would miss each other. They married me off and started planning the invitations to my wedding. Some urged me to pray more and praise God, while others invited me to imagine erotic escapades that contained neither prayers nor praise.

Such were the small, impossible dreams of the souls around me. In my liberation, they saw the fulfillment of their own deferred hopes. I had to listen to strange and bizarre dreams, when all I could see was their impossibility. I was incapable of believing, for I came from the generation of the lying gods, the generation of those whose dreams don't come true. I listened to people's dreams, and I practiced my expert skills at lying. I played along with the marriage fantasies. I worshipped alongside those who saw my good fortune as a confirmation of their faith. I practiced these lies and many others, and they helped me pass the weeks until it was time for the second group.

In October 2013, the names of the second group were announced, including five old souls from our prison block. For a second time, we witnessed a scene of farewell, as well as consolation from the new souls for those of us whose joy was postponed to the later groups. I kept climbing my mountain, and my stone was ready to tumble down each time for yet another ascent.

Family visits began taking on an exhausting, painful nature. My mother kept asking why her joy was delayed after she had gotten the house ready and decorated every corner. What about the new bed she had purchased from some of her friends? Why was I so slow to return to her? Did I want my features to fade from her mind? My mother did not stop with her questions, and in the end, they morphed into accusations: "Why are you still hanging there, my son? All the doors of heaven have been opened except yours. Damn your stone!

And damn the mountain peaks you have climbed! How can you bear to keep your mother waiting? How long will you ignore her embrace? People who were your companions in prison until only yesterday visit my home and tell me you are doing well, but I don't believe their lies about you. I received them at the door in case I might catch a hint of your smell upon them. They kissed my head and my hand, and I wished I was kissing you. You told me to pray more, so I did. You told me to trust in the mercies of the Lord, so I trusted. You told me not to die, so I've hung on. You said that I am the companion of all your tribulations, so why are you slow to join me in mine? When will you quit your lies, O fruit of my narrow womb and my milkless breast? You are your mother's stone, and you are the mountain... What a sadist of a child! Won't you have mercy on a mother tormented by your absence?"

My mother drew up all the charges she had prepared throughout two decades of pain. She added her journeys and the humiliations suffered at checkpoints. She added her hunching back and her failing eyesight. She added all my ghosts that kept her company in her solitude. She began surrendering, though no white flags proclaimed her decision. In her despair, she continued censuring me until my strength finally failed. I leapt from my wall and surrendered all my defenses to my mother's despair. I put on the clothes I was saving for my return to her. Together we spun the songs of our reunion and put sheets on the new bed. I returned to my old lies: "Just a few months, Mazyouna... It's not yet time to give up... One final stage, and we shall reach the end of the long road..." Together with other lies that my mother believed until, at last, she abandoned her questions and furled the flag of surrender once again. For the thousandth time, my mother believed my lies and returned home. She hung her dreams upon a wide banner and called upon her Lord for the final time, praying for a new day.

At the end of December 2013, to mollify public opinion, Israel declared it would build one hundred new housing units on occupied territory in exchange for each prisoner who was released. It was an astonishing price, but the old souls did not expend much effort trying to ignore it, nor did it kill their joy. The names of the next group were announced, including four of the old souls among us in Hadarim. They spoke many words of farewell to us, but said little that related to the walls.

A fourth and final group remained: thirty old souls. Still hanging, but with one last chance. Sterile negotiations between the two sides. A shameful American bias toward the Israeli position, accompanied by political pressure upon the Palestinians to force additional months of negotiations. Days and weeks passed heavily as the thirty old souls kept waiting, including the three with me. Winter intensified the cold of waiting, and it nearly froze the families of those souls. My latest lies kept my mother warm as she waited impatiently for each hour to elapse. Meanwhile, I kept hanging on to my wall, holding even tighter in my fear of the disappointments I sensed were approaching with swift, confident steps. I rose every morning and hoisted my stone. I kept each appointment with my mountain.

February breathed its last. The faces of the remaining names showed their anxiety as they waited for what might be their last chance at life beyond the wall. The Occupying State appeared to be procrastinating in their fulfillment of the appointed terms of the agreement. Palestinian leaders made no appropriate response. The tension had never been higher than on the day before the fourth and final group was scheduled to be released. A premature hereafter: that's what I saw in the scene of the thirty of us hanging eternally upon our walls. It was the day of judgment, followed either by life or else an appointment with an eternal wall of fire. The arrival of the hereafter was presaged by no signs or omens. It offered no opportunity for a final prayer, no time for repentance to wipe away some ancient sin.

My wall and I stood naked at the checkpoint: sometimes I sought protection behind it, and sometimes it hid behind me. With each step, we clung tighter to each other and reconfirmed our old covenant. The crossing guards interrogated us, mocking our nakedness and our fear of the gate. We proclaimed ourselves ready to let everything go and hold fast to the here and now. A life sentence might be the heavy stone that deprives you of every opportunity for resurrection and new life. A life sentence might be the mountain that refuses to bend down before your exhaustion. It might be all things, for things are what we want them to be.

The next day arrived, but no announcement came with it. Israel abandoned its commitment and held fast to the thirty remaining souls. The door was slammed in our faces, along with every possibility of escape to a time that would put an end to our hanging. We returned to our walls with nothing to wait for but our next hour in the sun.

According to Greek mythology, Adonis did not escape the tusks of his boar, which stood over him as he bled. The hunter fell; the prey triumphed. The beast did not rend the body of

Adonis but allowed him to bleed out slowly. Adonis prayed his final prayer and hung from the wall of his death. When Aphrodite arrived, too late, all that remained of Adonis was his cold body and his still-warm blood. Weeping, Aphrodite spun the threads of her beloved's blood into red flowers. Pluto watched Aphrodite weaving the red threads. Then he decreed: "Each spring and summer you will be resurrected, Adonis, to live your life on earth. But every fall and winter, I will bring you back to the underworld to die, along with all the plants of the earth." Pluto watched my return, and he arranged my fates as he saw fit. Who knows? Perhaps the next Aphrodite will not arrive too late to stanch the streaming blood.

From upon my wall, my Lord, the God of all the worlds, arranged a new appointment somewhere on planet Earth. Far from my bleeding and my wall, a new goddess was born. At her birth, she possessed a distant memory of an old boar, and when she grew up, she traced the threads of blood. She packed up her foreign alphabet and traveled to a land redolent of her parents' secrets. She lived several heartbeats away from my wall. She picked up the first thread of blood. With it, she began spinning for me and for her. She spun her spring and summer; she spun my autumn and winter. Her name was Nanna, the final goddess of love, and what comes next is my story with her.

PART TWO

Me, My Heart, and a Most Confining Place

Nanna

By some divine providence that I am unable to explain or fathom, it all began in the narrow space of time before the scheduled release of the final group of prisoners. I was hanging upon my wall, resisting the temptation to surrender and jump. I sought the lies that would console me in the face of my mother's insistent questions, which weighed upon my mind for hours. I ignored the other souls as they suffered through the remaining time to wait. Each of the thirty old souls sought a familiar corner to nurse a wound both new and very deep. I did not search long, nor did I hurry to treat my wound. I bridled my expectations and plunged deeper into my reading.

On the other side of the planet, Nanna was planning her first steps and picking up the first thread of blood. A child of the autumn like me, she was born in 1987 in one of the Mediterranean countries across the sea. That country lived among old legends of gods with strange names that did not easily fit inside her father's Arabic alphabet. Gods who flourished for thousands of years, and whose naked statues filled the cities as a testament to their eternal youth and wisdom.

Nanna believed some of the stories of the young gods, and she ignored the ones that surpassed her imagination with their talk of genealogies and soaring through the air. The diversity of languages in her small house astonished her. Even more was she astonished each time her parents succumbed to their longing and traveled from Italy to Palestine to renew old covenants with time and place. Nanna saw the other side of the sea. She observed another shade of blue. She tasted Eastern cooking, so spicy in its character and its scents. She met a grandfather in his seventies who responded to her interest with several cups of sugary tea. She listened without interest or understanding to grandmothers recounting their misfortunes.

Nanna filled her luggage with all the smells, colors, and images she could carry and returned to her naked statues and the ancient plazas that in their prime had welcomed returning conquerors, weighed down by the spoils of victory. Those same squares had received Saint Paul and the believers who were with him. They received Easterners who fell asleep as free men in the holds of ships and woke up as slaves of the people from the conquering shore. Nanna did not yet know the history of Rome's squares, nor was she interested in the revolutions of an East that was breaking away from a West exhausted by its victories.

The years grew within Nanna. Her parents tired of hearing stories of strange gods. They longed for stranger but more familiar gods. After ten years of exile and seeking their daily bread, they announced their surrender. Nanna packed her bags and returned to her old Mediterranean shore. Nanna returned for the sake of a last cup of her grandfather's tea before he breathed his last. She returned to city squares bare of statues and inscriptions, but crowded with people and faces that resembled old photos of her father. She returned to an air that crept in at night from the Jaffa shore and made its home inside the window of her room. She returned to her mother tongue, even though for years she had stammered when speaking it. Then she added the Hebrew language of the people who had descended suddenly and settled that land. It was a complicated alphabet for a child who had not yet passed her eleventh year. A language in which four diverse tongues, geographies, and cultures mixed together and found in Nanna their smallest common denominator.

When her school years ended, Nanna was still holding one end of the thread of blood. Her heart expanded, and its empty spaces were filled with the tempestuous desires of her femininity. Where now were the gods of love and beauty? Nanna despaired of the city squares around her, so narrow and empty of knights on white horses who had perfected the language of love in all four of its languages. She left home and moved to the big city to live in a student dormitory near the university, where she excelled in her studies.

Nanna continued to search for her knight, who was slow to answer her prayers. The adolescent knights she met, whose intact bodies were unmarked by either the injuries of victory or the pains of defeat, failed to win her heart with their chivalry and their simple flirtations. Nanna wanted something different, and she despaired of finding it. She earned a degree in restoring people's rights: a degree conferred by a university erected upon land that belonged to an old man until someone came to steal it to build their Jewish state. Nanna's studies came to an end, and she learned her lessons well. She memorized the features of that old man who died in exile, far from his land.

Nanna left the big city and returned to the cramped squares of her town, where she launched the first of her legal wars before a judiciary that legitimized its crimes through the courts. She fought long and hard, taking joy in small victories. Her opposition to the judiciary of the Occupying State increased as her awareness of its injustice grew. As the Occupying State hardened its policies toward the Palestinian minority, Nanna's questions about her identity became all the more insistent. She nearly found an answer, but my rising scream drew her attention to the thread of blood. She followed the thread as it twisted and turned among neighborhoods and alleys in various cities and towns, some depopulated by force and others that remained. Between the third group and fourth and final group, she followed that thread to the base of the wall. There the thread of blood came to an end, and there she began her first attempts to stanch its flow.

Nanna's first years after returning to her town, located within lands occupied in 1948, were accompanied by news and stories about an ancient wound that were recounted whenever families gathered and conversed. They told her about it often. She read about it everywhere. The details of the wound made their home in Nanna's psyche. She became so entangled that she decided to visit the clinic, pull back the bandages, and see the truth of what lay beneath.

As though passing that way for the first time, the streets closed in upon Nanna, and all her emotions were heightened. She approached Hadarim Prison and parked her car near the wall. She could feel the thread of blood getting warmer. After only a few cursory questions from the soldiers about her reasons for visiting, Nanna was inside the wall. She made her way through a space choked by doors and bars and the breath of soldiers. The guard escorting her gestured toward a small room labeled No. 6. Nanna entered and sat on a white plastic chair, facing a glass partition. After a few minutes, a wound arrived and sat down on a second white chair on the other side of the glass.

When the interview was over, that wound returned to the cellblock and talked about a young lady who had come to visit him. I listened to his excitement at the unexpected visit. Then we resumed waiting for the release date of the final prisoner group. One week later, Nanna came back for another visit. The wound had told her about two other wounds bleeding alongside it. After another week, Nanna came again, holding one end of a thread of blood in her hand. She met with the first wound, then the second. She sat on her chair and waited for the third and final wound, me.

I got dressed quickly and checked my shave in the mirror. Accompanied by a soldier, I proceeded a short distance until we stopped in front of room No. 6. The soldier opened the door and then locked it behind me.

There are some faces that surrender the key to their mysteries before finishing their first sentence. The next time you meet them, all that remains is a pale copy, with nothing left to provoke your anxiety, your instinct to search, or the tension that precedes the moment of discovery. Looking at such faces, you are able to notice peripheral details, such as the color of a dress and how it contrasts with the red of the lips, the style of the hair, and how the earrings hang down to brush against the neck. You notice details about the place, such as the color of the walls, the height of the ceiling, the number of light rays falling on the table between you. And then there is Nanna's face.

"Have mercy on these walls, young lady!" My first words went unheard by anyone but me, masked by the audible whispering of the walls. They had never before encountered anything like this figure's feminine confidence. I sat down on a white chair, across from Nanna in all her elegance. The glass partition between us did nothing to lessen the shock of what I was seeing. It was a face that told you nothing for free, revealed none of its secrets. A face that summoned you to set sail, to plunge deep, to keep searching. A face whose vanity would only be satisfied by taking your breath away. You call upon all your gods for help, yet you do not despair even when the riddle of that face unnerves your masculine self-confidence.

Time disappeared, place disappeared, Nanna's face remained. Present events evaporated, as did memories of the past, together with every voice and image they contained. Here was a face that promised nothing but exhaustion for whoever became entangled. A face you could not ignore, even when you closed your eyes. An enigma that combined the contradictions of East and West. I sat on my white chair and experienced Nanna's face.

"Hello."

"Hi."

"My name is Nasser."

"So they told me."

"Really!"

"I thought I would be meeting an old man."

"And indeed you are."

We talked a little about prison and about our wait for the final prisoner release. The atmosphere inside that small nook of a room was warm, and I could feel the ice melting. I ventured my first confession.

"Can I tell you something?"

"Of course."

"On the way here, I told myself that if it was a beautiful woman, I would stay for as long as I could, but if not, I'd keep things short and make a graceful exit after the fourth sentence."

"And what did you find?"

"I've just spoken my one hundredth sentence, and I'm still here," I said with a playful smile.

Her face echoed my smile, but it did not betray her impressions of my sudden candor. I liked the way she received my frankness. Her behavior suggested maturity in a woman who had not yet completed her twenty-seventh year. It increased my masculine curiosity, and I found myself transgressing the etiquette of a first meeting.

"How do you see the world, Nanna?"

My question took her by surprise. I could read the tension in her body as she struggled to find a suitable answer.

"What exactly do you mean?" She was attempting to buy time to find an answer to save herself. A smart play.

"Just what I said: What's your outlook on the world? Do you see it through a pessimistic lens, or from some other angle that minimizes its cares and pains?"

"I see it as it is."

We went on to speak about the sufferings of the world, about its poor and its lost. We spoke about wars, terrorism, and the occupation of our land. She volunteered basic information about her career in law and a little about her social circle. The visit ended, leaving each of us with a desire to talk longer. A soldier opened the door, and Nanna went out. Another soldier opened the door on my side and took me back to the cell. I changed into something more comfortable. I started thinking, dwelling upon the half hour that had brought me together with Nanna. Then I went back to my waiting and my wall.

Nearly a month went by. Nanna came back for a second visit, then a third. Both times, we had more to say about everything: her parents and eleven years of exile, her childhood in the shadow of the old Roman gods, her visit to Palestine, her grandfather and how close she felt to him, her return to the gods of her native country. We spoke about the camp, about exile, about dreams, about our wait for a final chance at freedom.

Over time, Nanna increased the frequency of her visits until she started coming every week. The conversations during our meetings were not enough, and we agreed to write letters in order to continue our dialogues, which branched out in every direction and delved ever deeper. Meanwhile, the Occupying State disavowed its obligations and refused to release the fourth and final group of prisoners. So I remained there, hanging upon my wall. My wound kept spilling blood, and its red threads twisted through Nanna's fingers. She kept spinning the threads, and I kept bleeding, waiting for her next visit or her first letter. Once again I embraced my life sentence. Once again I reconciled myself with hanging upon my wall to avoid every possibility of falling. Like someone beginning his detention all over again, I gathered my strength and hoisted my stone. No mountain would deny my insistence upon reaching my destination. I returned to my bleeding wound and refused to wait for it to be healed. I accepted the pain just as it was.

The next time, I walked so quickly that I startled the guard who escorted me. The soldier locked the door behind me. Nanna had not yet arrived. I sat on my white chair to wait. Before long I stood up, and in that instant Nanna came through the other door.

"Have I kept you waiting long?"

"No, I only just arrived."

"Are you well?"

"Now I am."

"Are you going to remain standing?"

"No. No, I'll sit."

I sat down, and a hush fell over our small nook. I broke the silence.

"What brings you back here, Nanna?"

"I don't understand."

"What brings you back to all this pain? Gods don't enter confined spaces. They try, but they fail when a feverish claustrophobia drives them off."

"I'm no goddess, Nasser."

"How do you know?"

"I'm here, and didn't you just say that gods don't enter confined spaces?"

"True, that's what I said, but you might be a goddess I haven't heard about."

"How much do you know of goddesses?"

"A lot."

"And do you believe in all of them?"

"I believe in the ones who don't look down on me when we talk."

An hour and a half went by, during which we discussed many things about world affairs and goddesses. The end of the visit was approaching.

"Nanna, describe for me a green space you passed on the way here."

"Do I absolutely have to?"

"Why do you ask?"

"Because I wasn't paying attention. But I promise to describe one for you next time."

I said what I always did at the end of our visits together: "Drive safe, Nanna."

"I will," replied Nanna, as she always did.

Nanna was away for two full weeks. What was happening to me? What exactly was I doing? What was it that was incessantly flirting with my hours? How did the days suddenly become so heavy? Where did my beautiful dream lovers go every night? What was this new waiting, which I did not understand, and which did not at all resemble my former waiting? Then the first of Nanna's letters arrived.

13 May 2014

My friend Nasser,

One day you asked me, "What brings you here? Why do you keep coming back? Are you a masochist? The gods themselves do not enter this place." I'm writing these lines to answer those questions for you, and for myself.

One day in March, as winter was coming to
an end, I came to this place and met someone who
told me that what he loved most were landscapes.
In today's world, these aren't the things that people
usually love or say are their favorite things. They aren't
something I thought about at all.

Today, I was on my way to a nearby village called
Jatt. It is situated on a hill running parallel to the
Apartheid Wall, across from two villages in the 1967
land, Zeita and Baqa ash-Sharqiyya. Heading north,
the road climbs the side of Mount Gerizim. Numerous
villages dot the upper slopes of this mountain. They
looked just as they had on other days after the sky has
showered them with the water of blessing and washed
away all the dust that can spoil the clarity of this view.
But now it looked like a painting. Suddenly it became
clear to me, my friend, that I was someone who loved
natural landscapes and just hadn't realized it yet. I
loved them instinctually, but without feeling that love,
and without enjoying it... That's the difference. You
feel this love. You know its proper value. As for me, I
loved without knowing the value of the things around
me. The concept of love in our world has changed, and
so has the meaning of things. We live in the time of
Facebook, smartphones, and advanced technology,
when everything is available at the touch of a button.
In order to enjoy our love for things, they have to be
three-dimensional and easy to grab onto.

I live in a time and place beset by the epidemic
of materialism. Breaking free from this illness is as

difficult as it is important. Everyone competes to be the best—to be the most distinguished in their material possessions and appearance—until this competition ends up making us all alike. Things have lost their value, even as they are labeled with prices that demand our attention. Many people don't know that beautiful things, the things that make you happy, are within everyone's reach. I didn't know that either, but I discovered it with your help. From now on, I will enjoy the landscapes that exist all around me. From now on, I will know that I love them, and the knowledge of that love will be enough for me to taste happiness, if only for a few seconds. Love for love's sake is the very definition of beauty.

This is only one small point in the sea of your words during a March visit that lasted under an hour. Now do you understand what keeps bringing me back? Perhaps this is a simple matter in your eyes, for you realize the value of things. But for me, the power of discernment has grown weak, and it needs reinforcing. It is only by losing something that we understand its value. You don't feel this sense of lack, so it's natural you wonder why I keep coming back. Don't worry! I'm no masochist. I'm a naturalist in an unnatural reality, and I need to meet supernatural people like you in order to preserve the balance of my nature.

So happy I've met you,
Nanna

* * *

As soon as I finished reading the letter, I immediately dashed off a quick reply, in which I warned Nanna about the dangers of becoming entangled with ancient pains that promised nothing but exhaustion. I could see her listening to my replies to her questions, becoming absorbed in the details without any sense of fear or alarm. She didn't hurry my answers along, nor did she interrupt when I dragged out my descriptions of life for the souls behind bars, upon the wall. This young woman had spent four years studying in a big city, living in a small apartment and learning about the souls in prison.

I went back to read the letter a second time. I let it go for several days. Then I read it a third time, and I felt a desire for even more of her words.

To Miss Someone

I stood in front of my mirror several minutes longer than usual, checking my shave a second time. I made sure my clothes looked right and no hair was out of place. Then I sat on my chair and waited for the guard to arrive. I was at a loss to explain the tension I felt. I was also at a loss to come up with any sentence to begin the conversation with Nanna. I wasn't normally like that. Every time I returned to the mirror, a bewildered face stared back at me. The soldier arrived. Walking fast; a door opening. Then I was seated on my white chair, with Nanna facing me through the glass. She looked more elegant than ever, and it was obvious that she had spent even more time than me in front of the mirror. But I did not spend too much time examining what she was wearing. How could I, in the presence of a face that caused even the walls of that little nook to stop and stare?

"Wow."

"You like my outfit?"

"Absolutely."

"Thank you."

"You came back."

"Won't I always?"

"So stubborn!"

"And have you stopped being so stubborn?"

"I fear what will happen if you get lost in our pain."

"When will you stop talking to me as though I'm some weak woman?"

"I'm not. And that's not what I meant."

"That's precisely what you're doing and what you meant. And I wish you'd stop talking about how much older you are than me."

"But I'm so old."

"Not at all. There's nothing about your age that frightens me."

When we left the nook, Nanna raced ahead and sat down on my bed. She watched me stagger back into the cell. None of my daily routines helped me to forget her presence. She inhabited every hour of my day. My wall was filled with news about her and with the features of a face I had come to know by heart. Hour by hour, my confusion demonstrated that I was a traitor, conspiring against my wall. The days passed slowly until Nanna's second letter arrived.

> My friend Nasser,
> It is 10:14 on the evening of Friday, 30 May 2014. In a little while, I'm off to bed because a long and difficult day of work awaits me. I'm looking around my small room. As I've told you before, it contains nothing but a bed, one small bookshelf, and another larger one. My diploma is on the wall, along with a flag of this country that exhausts you, but which you love anyway.

Since I still don't have a letter from you, I was forced to read your letter to my friend Magda. I no longer cared who it was addressed to. The words were yours, and that's all it took for them to have a deeper impact on me than anyone else's words could have. That's no flattery.

But I have something to tell you. That girl you claim has moved into a single apartment to live among souls in prison and the dead is the person most afraid of death. It took her so long to move into her own apartment because she feared being alone. She had already learned English by the time she left her parents' bed and started sleeping in her own room. That's how scared she was of monsters and thieves— even Father Christmas! That girl actually got her new apartment precisely to see beauty through you, Nasser. Before this recent move, she took no pleasure in the forms, colors, and beauty of nature. I think it was you who moved when you came to dwell in her eyes, which began to see beauty in a new light. I don't think that someone who has a motive for seeing life and beauty can possibly count as one of the prison souls or the dead. You are nothing but yourself. And didn't you say that a man never dies so long as he is present in the memory of a woman? If that's so, O master of contradictions, how can you be among the dead? Haven't you established your home in that girl's eyes? So don't try to frighten me with all this talk of the prison souls and the dead.

I will now go to sleep, completely happy and
content. But before doing so, I have a small confession
to make. I think my limited experience with the world
of men is the reason for that superficial comment
I made about men never feeling shy around other
people, and how I loved the image of a man full of
confidence and strength. Never in my life, Nasser,
could I imagine that a man's confusion in the presence
of a woman might make him more attractive. I will tell
you some other time what changed my mind...

I want to keep writing, but at law school they
taught us about the right of the accused to remain
silent. I think I've incriminated myself more than
enough for one letter! So,

May you wake to find every goodness,
Love, beauty, and color,
Life and the living,
Strength and freedom.

May God watch over you and keep you from every
harm.

From the one you claimed dwells with prison
souls and the dead,
Nanna

My waiting took on a hue that changed week by week. Either
a visit would increase my confusion and my entanglement
in Nanna's face, or else a letter would impel me to write a
quick reply, warning Nanna against getting too close, even

as I left the door open to any possible approach. I wrote my confusion and the chaos of my emotions. I wrote my desire to see her and read her more deeply. I wrote my fear of a great thing approaching, whose secrets I couldn't fathom. But I wrote with extreme caution. Suspicion and doubt, not only of Nanna but also of myself, could be read between the lines. In my writing, I disguised the mix of feelings that pervaded my mind, and none of them made it onto the page. But Nanna was less cautious than me, something she revealed in a third letter:

Nasser, no more tricks. Let me speak plainly. I won't call you "friend," but instead I'll call you "dear." Friendship usually implies the passage of time, but the affection found in "dear" might be born in an instant, and it only took an instant for me to lose myself under the force of your words. My intellect and every possible weapon have abandoned me, and I was left like an unarmed combatant. But the laws of physics don't lie, and as they say, every action has an equal and opposite reaction. And so, angry that our meeting was suddenly over, I departed with a further burst of energy and was compelled to discharge my emotions into this ink if I wanted to preserve the safety of those around me.

Dear Nasser, for me to be the person you meant by your last words is something that makes me proud, very proud—all in only a few words. I was able to grasp how rich you are in your words and your sensibilities. A genius, in fact. You are an innocent child, a mischievous youth, a perspicacious man, a responsible combatant, and a romantic lover, all at the same time. You have an exceptional ability to evoke beauty with your words, to transmit your love to things despite all the darkness that surrounds us. That is probably what made me doubt, when we first met, that you had passed your forty-fourth year. I insisted you had to be younger. People get old when they stop loving, and you still have an exceptional capacity to love. Because I love to profit (in the purely capitalistic sense of the word) and to benefit others, you absolutely must write more so that I can bring your words to the outside. Let me spread this disease so I'm not the only one who's infected! Every time I read your words, and after every visit, I feel I have grown more mature, and that my knowledge of the things around me has deepened. For that, I owe you so much.

I possess no linguistic ability such as yours, and my words are inadequate to describe the stage I'm now passing through. You possess depth and sensitivity, wisdom and strength, desire and freedom and imagination and perception and manliness. How rare for all those elements and descriptions to be found in a single person! No wonder you've brought me up short.

My dear, there's one thing you still lack— recognizing that perfection is God's alone—and that is for you to be convinced that I'm not a masochist. All this is just my reaction to a powerful and awesome action. I will tell you about it some other time, because I've already taken too much of your time.

I warn you that I am very stubborn. Your promise to give me a tour of Bethlehem still stands, and I'll hold you to it. If it turns out that all this is just a passing dream, then at the very least you absolutely must promise me it is a dream shared between us.

Your partner in dreaming… and in a partnership
forced upon you,
Nanna

For my part, I kept up my trickery despite my entanglement, which began expanding until it encompassed my walls. This was a different kind of waiting, and I liked it. It was as though my life sentence had not begun all over again just yesterday when the fourth group wasn't released. I wrote more letters, and I addressed Nanna in every kind of indirect language. Sometimes I warned her to keep away, other times I flirted with her about her next visit. My question about what to do faded away, and Nanna's face remained before me as the sole answer.

I saw Nanna leave our nook as though she were being torn away by force. She fought for every minute in order to hear just a few more words, and I certainly wasn't stingy with my speech. After every meeting, I tore down another bridge that connected me to my life as it existed before her. It wasn't a conscious decision but rather a submission to a greater force that shook half of everything I used to know. The prisoners around me noticed the flow of letters coming from Nanna. So did the guards. But no one said anything. Nanna, on the other hand, had much to say in her next letter.

7 June 2014

My dear Nasser,

This essay of mine goes back to February 2010. At that time, I was more and more convinced I would never find the person I wanted to share my life, my days, and my dreams with. My conviction was a bulwark against my friends' claims that I was hard to please and needed to lower my standards a little. Honestly, ever since that time, I promised myself I would never allow such accusations to affect me or my decisions. I had forgotten all about this essay until I was reminded of it when speaking to your niece Shatha about Jaffa and the sea there. I went digging through boxes and searching my journals. I don't know why, but I felt a strong desire to send it to you without saying anything about it beforehand. Actually, that's not true. I know exactly why I wanted to do that, but I'm going to keep hiding the reason to avoid becoming more involved.

Here I am, O Jaffa Sea!

I've slipped away from my everyday life and have come to you in the utmost secrecy, as though this were some illicit affair. How could our meeting not be a sin?! I felt your call this morning. I was sleeping when the sun's rays suddenly tickled my face, stealing through a window that is my portal onto paradise. After days of long, heavy rain, when I did not come for fear of seeing you in a foul mood, I immediately responded to the sun's invitation. I skipped my lectures, ditched my friends, and left behind my phone along with everything else that might violate the sanctity of our time together. I love seeing you at your most beautiful. You preserve my hope that I'll find a soul to soar away with me into the clouds. Now I've come, wanting you to overwhelm me as no one has ever done. I am certain someone will cross my path soon, someone like you who will take me off to the distant horizons stretching out before me. Don't make fun of me! I sometimes feel lost, and I no longer understand who I am. Am I dreaming? Am I being too demanding or hard to please? Or maybe I'm just lost, or a realist, or just silly. I don't know.

All I do know is that I want him to be like you. For his existence to shatter me, for his waves to sweep me away from afar. I want him to be deep like you, with riches deep and obscure. I will discover them gradually, so that the excitement never eases. He will reveal his pages, one after another, and take pleasure in arousing me and stimulating my thoughts.

Now I hear the muezzin calling the afternoon prayer from the mosque by the sea. Despite all the reminders of Zionism imposed upon me in this place, the sound of the waves intertwines with the call to prayer to produce a particular splendor. Even if you do not perform the prayer, this magical atmosphere diffuses so much peace and calm.

I want him to be like you. An Eastern seashore, even if his breezes come from the West. A color reminiscent of this soil. Lines on his face that echo these rocks. A master

*of its language, knowing its madness. I want him to stand
as tall as the minaret of this ancient, resilient mosque,
despite being surrounded by strange people. I want him to
be like the bells of that church, which keep him company
in exile.*

*O Jaffa Sea, you remain a symbol of this hope. You
preserve my certainty that I will find him, wherever he
may be. He will be my miracle. He will be the colors of
my life and the painter who paints them. I will whisper in
his ear an eternal secret when I tell him, "You alone shall
discover my weak spots. I hand you the reins of my spirit.
Before you, I strip off all my feigned strength and sink into
your depths, surrendering my very last breath."*

Dear Nasser, I reveal to you—you alone!—my
weak spots. I wish you a happy day, a peaceful day,
just like that day I had on the shore of the Jaffa Sea,
a day full of hope like that one in March, when the
negotiations were taking place and I met a soul like
a sea breeze in my life. I'm showing the first signs of
getting involved. I don't want to hide them—nor to
catch you off guard.

Nanna

What an impossible clash this was! How was I to measure
up to the Jaffa Sea, a godfather who could provide an infin-
ity of possible answers to a young woman in her early twenties, who revealed her deepest secrets as she stood before the

waves? Nanna was abandoning her sea and making me the wellspring of her answers. Did Nanna know what a heavy responsibility she was laying upon the shoulders of a man whose strength was already exhausted by the weight of his stone? Would my wall be able to endure new complications on top of the old ones?

It was 18 June 2014. Nanna was sitting on her chair. I said nothing, overwhelmed by the power of her face. A face that gives you a thousand reasons to live and keeps you from dying, even when it's death that you long for. Then I spoke, and I said a lot. Nanna looked as elegant as ever, but I could not focus on any details beyond the outline of her face. I spoke like someone hiding a secret from her and from myself.

"What brings you here today?"

"Aren't you glad I came?"

"It's not that, but we were supposed to meet tomorrow."

"I know."

We went back to our long conversations about everything. We spoke about Jaffa and the sea there. I hid how lost I felt. I hid the heavy questions that were weighing me down. Nanna talked about the legal case that had been assigned to her, and her joy at an appeal that had restored some rights to an old man. I rejoiced too, even happier than she. The visit was coming to an end. Nanna stood up and looked at me like someone seeing me for the first time.

"Do you want to know why I came today instead of tomorrow?" she asked abruptly.

"Yes, absolutely."

She was silent for a while, looking at me intently.

"Because I missed you."

A guard opened the door on Nanna's side, and she went out. I rose to my feet but just stood there, trying to rearrange the words that had come out of Nanna's mouth into some language I could comprehend. The soldier interrupted my linguistic processing and took me back to my cell. Nanna departed to her seashore with her old questions, leaving me to plunge into the very lowest of my depths. Nanna knew exactly what she was saying. She carefully chose the time and place to shoot her first arrow. Then she left before confirming whether it had struck a lethal blow or had merely grazed me, leaving me alive until her next visit. Nanna began spinning the streaming threads of my blood. She spun them in her own way, and who can blame a goddess for her actions? To miss someone. A liminal phrase, whose borders you stumble across at the very moment you are most lost. There are a thousand ways to miss someone. Which interpretation of the word would save me from a week of pondering its meaning? How could I believe in my victory over the sea when my dry ground contained nothing but my wall and my old stories with their antiquated words? Why was I behaving so moderately, when I was the one who had been provoked, sometimes severely, by Nanna's questions throughout the past months? The questions kept coming until another letter arrived from Nanna.

Friday, 20 June 2014

My small room, under a white ceiling where we've drawn imaginary timelines of the evening we spent together, listening to the melodies of an oud piece played by Le Trio Joubran, accompanied by the voice of Mahmoud Darwish. That song touches the depths of my soul and leaves me with you in a paradise. I knew some features of that heaven before you came, without knowing that you would complete whatever had been missing. This harmony between a piece I've always loved and the way you play in my imagination right now dazzles me so much that I wonder if you've always been up there on the ceiling, and I somehow missed it.

But since you're not sitting in front of me now as I'm writing these stupid confessions, I'll be braver and say your presence is not limited to the ceiling of my bedroom. You're with me everywhere. When I visit the ruins of the village of Tantura to see the traces of a wound that has not yet healed, it's the same wound I read in your eyes. And when I go to Mount Carmel, which once burned with holy fire, and I see how beautiful it still is despite the blackness of the world, then I see you. The roses in the Bahá'í Gardens confirm that you paint the most vivid colors in my life. The sea makes me feel how powerfully you wash over me. You tower before me like Mount Gerizim, and when the breeze touches my cheek, I feel your gentle caress. I visit the depopulated village of Qaqun so that you and I might keep alive the memory of its fall by singing the Palestinian national anthem over its lands. I praise God a thousand times over for the blessing of sunglasses, which hide you from the gaze of others when tears gather in my eyes.

Nasser, don't laugh. I'm taking your advice when
I open my closet to pick out the clothes I'll wear when
I visit you. You made things very hard when you said
white looks good on me! I'm thinking back to the time
I took a risk and told you I missed you. I didn't know if
you would judge me, and if so, what you would think.
Yet it was no secret, despite my best efforts to hide it.
I'm no good at hiding the truth—nor do I want to be.
And apparently, Nasser, the truth of the matter is that
you've thrown me in over my head, and I can't swim
back to shore.

                                        Nanna

Here was Nanna addressing me, addressing all of me. She was
using the walls and ceiling to draw my story. That was her first
experience of hanging upon my old wall. Welcome, Nanna, to
the world of the people of the sky! Are you still good at soaring, or have you spent so long on the ground that you believe
in the law of gravity?

Because I Love You

On 24 June 2014, Nanna could sense my impatience and shortened my wait by coming one day early. When the guard closed the door behind me, Nanna was already sitting on her chair, watching me and trying to read my face as I kept my silence. I pulled out a slip of paper that I had hidden from the guard. I pressed the paper to the glass so Nanna could read the question I had written for her: "On your last visit, you said you missed me. Do you know what those words mean in the language of the people of the sky?"

Nanna looked straight into my eyes and nodded. We sat there without saying a word. I don't know which of us broke the silence.

"Don't worry about my feelings toward you. Just say what you're feeling."

"If only things were that simple, Nanna!"

"Say anything. I'm a grown woman. I can handle it."

"Nanna, look at me. Look close."

"That's all I've been doing for months, Nasser. I'm looking at you."

"I have nothing to offer you except my life, my bonds, and my life sentence."

"I know this trinity of yours. I'm coming to you despite it. I'm coming to you because of it."

"I'm scared about you getting involved in this enormous mountain of pain."

"Don't be scared for me. Not while I'm with you."

"But I'm afraid for you on my account."

"Nasser, stop pushing me away. Just tell me something."

"What do you want me to say?"

"Tell me what you want. Whatever it is."

I talked to Nanna about things growing inside me despite myself. I talked about our first meeting, our second, our ninth. About her dwelling in my wall, about my becoming entangled in her face, about my waiting for her visit, about the weight of the hours, about watching her approach, about my desire for her to come closer, about my fear of getting close. I talked to her about my fear for her on account of me, my prison, and her youth compared to my advancing years.

"Why all this fear for me?"

For a moment, I didn't breathe. I didn't search for an answer that would save us both. I didn't examine my options. There wasn't time for anything between her question and me.

"Because I love you."

Four and a half decades, the first half of which I had spent before a wall that imposed upon me the refugee's crisis of the camp. It was a transparent life, hiding nothing and afflicted by the abundant curses of angry gods. A childhood that went hungry until it found something to fill its belly. A father whose back was bent when poverty broke his manhood. A mother in poverty who struggled to dig a well so long that her limbs dried up and snapped. A fearful, hesitant, and idle adolescence. A confused youth, pursued by some of the camp's women, who inscribed upon his body their own desire for disobedience and rebellion. Then young adulthood, during which I learned every manner of falsehood, turning my lies into a legend that would be told and sung. My university years expanded my consciousness, even as they made me feel like an exile by denying me and my story.

As for the second half of my life, those decades were spent behind a wall erected upon my desire and upon my wound. The wall clung to me with a lover's embrace, and it flirted as fiercely as a couple in the first days of their love. It ate my flesh and my bones. It expanded and contracted however it wished. It never once opposed me or resisted my plunge into its vast spaces. It scolded if I shifted my position, hanging there upon it, and it pardoned me whenever I became silly. It endured the pain of wounds that stuck to the mattress and disturbed its midday nap. It stayed up until the last wound slept, when it would come to cry over my bleeding.

Languages, nationalities, and religions intermingled upon my wall. So did lovers, the scent of their perfume, and the remains of clothes they left behind on my bed. It declared that many of my strange acts were permissible, and it explained away many of the Qur'an's verses about forbidden things. The wall hid me from life even as it hid life from me. When I was weak, it was gentle in its rebukes.

My wall foretold Nanna's coming. It began preparing me to meet another world, a world hidden from me for two decades and more, even as I was hidden from it. In my naivete, I thought my youthful years behind the camp's walls had been intended to prepare me, with the wisdom of providence, for

what lay ahead: my life sentence, hanging upon a second
wall. That's what I kept thinking up until Nanna appeared
in three dimensions, seated upon her white chair behind the
glass wall. Throw away your stone, Sisyphus, for your great
mountain has been made low within you. Leave behind your
wound, Adonis, for your bleeding has not yet begun.

"Because I love you." All the previously unspoken words
and their meanings jumped out to form the fate that had fun-
damentally altered the scene inside the small nook where
Nanna and I met. If only she had been content to alter that
room alone! For there was nothing in my entire existence,
neither on earth nor in heaven, that didn't wear a new aspect,
never before known…In that moment another country, from
another time, amid an entirely new nature, took shape for us.

"Because I love you." I could see a woman in a royal-red
dress sitting to my left, playing a cello. The neck of the cello
climbed up her breast and caressed her neck with a gentle-
ness at odds with her playing. The woman felt no shame at
revealing two marble legs, showing even more of her thighs
than was necessary and agitating me profoundly. She played
without asking permission, caring nothing for my taste in
music or my ancient Eastern disposition. She played upon my
strings, and her Western music spoke to my confusion and
my tension. I didn't dare reveal what I was seeing and hearing, for Nanna wouldn't have understood the madness of the
threads I was spinning. Yet there was nothing in the music
or in the musician that could detract from my amazement
over Nanna. From both sides of the glass partition, she and I
quickly became part of the same scene. My own music did not
form the soundtrack for what was happening. Instead, Nanna

brought her own music with her. Indeed, she was the music that played behind everything that took place and was said.

"Because I love you." I don't know why, but a scene from the movie *Notting Hill* came to mind. The heroine of the film stands before the one she loves and asks how he is. His wound is so fresh that it colors the pages of the books that line the shelves of his bookshop. Without meaning to, she has broken his heart, and he sought to heal his wound in a small library nook, sought to let go of all of his hanging upon her as he grasped at another possible salvation. Now she stands before him, surrounded by books. She despairs that the threads of his blood will ever respond to her spinning, but she tries one last time and says, "I'm just a girl, standing in front of a boy, asking him to love her." Nanna's spinning and her music brought that scene to life at that moment, in that nook, behind that wall.

"Because I love you." All the walls around me became transparent, revealing their secrets. Nothing was concealed from me; nothing concealed me. I saw the soldiers standing behind the walls, Nanna's car beside the wall, the green fields that Nanna often forgot existed, the Apartheid Wall a little to the north in the occupied West Bank, the military check-points everywhere, the air of my country with its ancient smell, boys and girls with no future, half-freedoms distributed like false promises that everyone believes. I saw all the roads that took me to Nanna's house. I saw the ruins of Palestinian villages, buried under the Occupation's villages and towns. I saw the cities built on the beach along the sea...

God opened all the gates to his gardens. It was as though someone addressed me and said, "This is what you abandoned when you began hanging upon your wall! But now, here is

Nanna in front of you. Come out of your old wounds and plant a new field of wounds upon her lips. This is Nanna in front of you, asking you to love her. For shame! How can you tarry with your steps and your kisses? What impotence nails you in place? Stretch out your hand, or something more. This is the last and most beautiful thing the world will offer you. It joins all you have forgotten with all you still remember."

"Because I love you." I looked back: My hanging and my falling off the wall, my confinement and constriction: it all returned. Nothing was concealed from me, and nothing concealed me. God opened all the gates of His hell. Nothing would save me now from burning in Nanna. I fell from my wall, and it fell from me. I released my grip, and the wall let me go. The glass wall opened every eye I had closed, and I was unable to resist. The world came to me with the best, the most beautiful, the sweetest thing it had, placing it on the chair before me. Nanna. She was all the temptations of heaven and earth and what lies between. Things forbidden by God and his prophets—though in her, all things were permissible. Nanna was the road to heaven for those who pray. She was the answer to all the questions.

"Because I love you." Each of us sat upon our chair, checking to make sure our souls had survived the passage. We spoke many words about love, and love took an even deeper hold upon us. Nanna's face remained the sole fixed point in the midst of everything I could see through the transparent walls. Nanna became my sole certainty, my only safe refuge, now that I had let go of my wall and left it behind.

I told Nanna about the cello player and about *Notting Hill*. I told her many other things. Nanna responded creatively to my madness.

"I love you."

"I love you more."

"If only there were more, Nanna! I would keep piling it up until I drowned."

"I would sink further into you."

"I will miss you."

"Me too."

"I don't want to leave."

"I want to stay here forever."

"Tell time to stop."

"I'll do it."

"Drive safe, Nanna."

The guard escorted me back to my cell with its transparent walls, which had abandoned their task of concealing me and protecting me. Nanna accompanied me, as though knowing how much I needed her company. She beat me there and sat on my bed. She made me coffee and lit my first cigarette with me... This was Nanna, a goddess of confined places and the goddess of me.

I failed in my fight against pen and paper. Everything inside me wanted to write to Nanna and say: "This is me, Nanna. I don't have anything apart from myself, my bonds, and my life sentence." I wanted to repeat it time after time in Nanna's ears. I wanted to be sure that is what she saw sitting in front of her on the white chair. I picked up my pen and wrote.

> I believe... that I am alive though dead, free though a prisoner. I am a young man in his midforties. I am a martyr in my paradise, without any wine or heavenly nymphs.

I believe... in God, the Lord of shackles and chains, the
   Lord of hunger, wars, and earthquakes, the Lord of
   the living and the dead, the Lord of the poor, and the
   Lord of the middle class.

I believe... in all God's messages, both heavenly
   and earthly. I read the Qur'an, the Torah, and the
   Gospel. Together with Moses, I carried the Ten
   Commandments, and then twenty more.

I believe... that my life sentence has not yet begun, that
   my sky is thunder and lightning, that my mother has
   stopped counting, and that my father died a defeated
   man, with no one to pray over him or mourn him
   with a funeral procession.

I believe... that Palestine is my passion, my Algiers, and
   my Damascus, that Yarmouk is freed, that return is a
   right, and that Jerusalem is captured in the eyes of the
   drunks and those who pray.

I believe... that women are the guardians of men, that Eve
   was innocent of our banishment from paradise, that
   our fates are forged by our own hands, that the apple
   was permissible, and I was the first to take a bite.

I believe... that borders are heresy, that racial and sexual
   discrimination is a delusion, that the Inquisition was
   false, and that freedom of speech and action is not
   just a right but is morality and religion.

I believe... that the walls of the cell are real, that my
   chains are iron, that my wrist is firm, and that my
   visitor with the Eastern face does not forget, nor will
   she compromise, and that she was born from the very
   womb of October.

I believe...that my poverty is wealth, that my
    bachelorhood is yearning, and that my orphanhood
    is a shinbone; that the mythical Buraq took me to my
    father one night; and that if you die, Mother, you will
    have betrayed my heart.
I believe...that the one sleeping in my breast is a child,
    that breaking hearts is murder, that love comes first
    and remains for good, and that the one who once
    loved me has forgotten.
But woe unto you! For how could you forget!

I had nothing to offer apart from what I declared: words, a
journey, a long hanging, stories about old walls and some
other new ones. In Nanna, I did not only find someone to
love. I found in her a companion for my mission and for the
journey. A partner for the shared causes and interests that we
made into our song and our treatise during weekly meetings
and our letters. My words had to be enough for Nanna. Likewise, my spiritual participation in her hours and her days. I
dwelt wherever she trod, and I stayed up to watch as she
slept. I sat beside her every time she thought she was alone. I
kissed her at the start of each morning as we drank our coffee
together. I kissed her in the middle of the day, and at the fall of
every night, I returned to finish what we had begun. I wanted
to be sure of my presence throughout her day exactly as I was
sure of her presence through all my hours. Geography disappeared. Borders disappeared. I no longer struggled to conjure
up Nanna's presence, for she had descended into my cell and
decided never to leave. I couldn't accept anything less than a
similar presence in her life.

28 June 2014

My beloved Nasser,

Tomorrow is the first day of Ramadan. I felt
a strong desire to send my holiday greetings, even
though I know we have never spoken about fasting.
But someone told me you fast for Ramadan and
would also be praying. That gladdened my heart, for
you know now how much I love the way the Jaffa Sea
harmonizes with the call to prayer. I was also struck
by a desire to send my greetings to your mother, Aunt
Mazyouna. Maybe because I know how deeply you
love her and admire her. When I speak with her, I feel I
am communicating with you, and I embrace her voice
and her lavish invocations with all my heart.

2 July 2014

Here you are, upon my white ceiling, as I prepare
myself to conjure you up so we can spend some time
together, if only for a few moments that are worthy
of the magic that floats around us. I don't feel sleepy
yet, for I am still reviewing everything that happened
during our meeting, still trying to comprehend your
ability to encompass me and touch my core. I can't
understand how you can possibly believe you are able
to cause me any pain or suffering... Someone like
you, Nasser, is incapable of hurting me. That's not
your nature. Today, I read your poem "I Believe" to
my mother, who hadn't known about us till now. Her
reaction was extremely positive. Well, I'm starting
to get tired, and I think I'll go to bed. If you come to

tuck me in, I might whisper in your ear how deeply wrapped up in you I am, and how I will never stop loving you.

3 July 2014

I spent the evening sitting with the members of my family, listening to them talk. But I wasn't really listening. Through all that time, I was suffering from a desperate need for you. I tried to bring back that moment when I was gazing at you and you told me you wanted us to stay like that for five minutes. I regretted not doing it, not submitting to your eyes. All I feel now is my desire to surrender, and this feeling is a lesson not to feel so constrained the next time. I've just scrolled through Facebook. All the news was bad, especially the news about the martyrdom of Mohammed Abu Khdeir. I looked online for *Notting Hill*, and it wasn't hard to find. I'll leave you now, and we'll be together again soon!

Nanna

Speaking of Love

I replaced all nouns with "Nanna." "I" became "we." Individual actions in my lexicon became collective ones: We got up late and washed our faces. We prepared our morning coffee, and we jumped up from breakfast when too many people disturbed the morning calm. We fixed our clothes, and then we stood before the mirror again, taking satisfaction in how we looked. We read the newspapers, even though they only made us more depressed with all the news about killing, starvation, and exile. We burned up our depression with a second cigarette. We went outside for our hour of sunshine and caught the tail end of someone explaining people's dreams from the previous night. We expounded our political and social analyses, and we offered a number of progressive ideas that displeased some of the more conservative souls. Standing apart, we burned during that hour in the sun until our bodies darkened—or whatever skin we revealed, anyway, and Nanna always revealed more than me. Our hour in the sun ended, and we returned to our cells. We sat down for a while to rest and swapped news with the fellow souls. We read politics or history or literature. We watched a boring film about the Second World War. Then came the second hour outdoors before the sun went down, followed by a second return to the cell.

After sunset, Nanna and I waited for the evening meal to arrive. We ate quickly, without tasting the food. Then we killed time until our fellow souls in the cell set about their private business so that we could again be alone together.

My wall retained not even the least part of its former compassion. It seemed to be avenging my betrayal, now that I was no longer hanging upon it. By looking through the wall, I could see every possible or probable life, in every shade and hue. Life crept on in every direction beyond my transparent wall. Souls that resembled us raced through their hours. Streets and vehicles never ceased their motion. Green spaces dwindled in front of concrete monstrosities that rose up and marched across the earth.

Nothing veiled me any longer. That was my wall's revenge. More than twenty years of hanging upon it did me no good. I was afraid, but I did not apologize. My wall turned its back on me. It scolded and threatened.

"How could you fall?"

"I grew tired."

"Do you believe what you see beyond me?"

"I believe in Nanna."

"I carried you for a thousand years and a day."

"Haven't you consumed enough of my flesh?"

"Pick up your stone, Nasser. Beyond me lies only the mountain."

"But before me, I see only Nanna."

"These aren't your old lies. How can you believe them?"

"Haven't you seen Nanna's face?"

My wall fell silent and didn't address me further. That was our last conversation. I cajoled it long and often, but my wall continued to take revenge in silence.

Beyond the transparent wall, God awakened all his creatures, even those dead and extinct. He restored nature to its roots. He brought back the earthquake, the volcano, and the flooding river. He increased the thirst of death and its strange, uncertain times. I grew afraid again. I cursed the crowded roads every time Nanna left me and went to her car. Whenever Nanna thought about going on a trip, I cursed the Wright brothers, with their iron monsters that filled the sky. Everything made me afraid for Nanna. I couldn't bear the idea of anything happening to her, no matter how minor. My wall didn't stop punishing me. Nanna was the bubbling spring of my fear, but she was also my safe zone and the source of my strength. She was my doubt; she was my certainty. She was my sea; she was my shore. I fled from her to her, and my final battle was in her. I decided I would be victorious, for no lover can ever be defeated after spending a single night beside Nanna and waking up to her eyes.

Nanna and I continued our weekly meetings in our nook, accompanied by the cello player. I did not articulate my fears to Nanna. I needed more time to explore the contours of this new field of battle in order to become perfectly confident of my victory. I had not been victorious in all my battles, but I never once fled a confrontation that chose me, or that I chose. In my battle for Nanna, I was victorious, dead or alive. I triumphed, but that did not prevent me from fearing for Nanna and warning her. Being killed meant nothing to me, though I was terrified that she'd be killed—or else the dreams I'd hung upon the glass wall in our nook would be.

"What is she wearing?" Nanna was asking about the cellist.

"I didn't notice."

"Feel free to look."

"You're sure?"

"Yes."

"She's wearing a red dress."

"And what is she playing?"

"Something new. But it suits us."

"She's smart then too."

"Are you jealous?"

"Yes, of everything you see or touch."

"I see only you."

"So much the worse for you!"

"You're beautiful even when you threaten."

"It's you who makes me like that."

"Don't close every door, Nanna. How will you get away from all this?"

"Are we back to that again?"

"And again and again."

"Why can't you just give it up?"

Nanna spun more threads. She spoke about the life to come. She built herself a house. She chose the colors of the flowers in her little garden. She cooked delicious dishes. She turned down the lights in the dining room and let me choose the music. She picked out a romantic movie for us to watch and laid her head on my shoulder. She cried at the scene of parting. (She had cried at the scene of meeting too.) She got up to check on our daughter Salma and her little dreams. She pressed her lips against Salma's forehead. Then she came back to tempt my fatigue with the kisses that always started her night.

Nanna spun many plans. She grew upset that I stuck to our small nook and insisted on soaring only through its vast narrow space. I wanted her to see me: to see me, my bonds, and my life sentence, and not to forget who I was, not even for a moment. This was me. This is how I introduced myself. Her dreams showed me nothing new. My diaphanous wall had already laid out the details of every possible dream. But I ignored what it offered. I let go of all its possibilities and held fast to Nanna, my one sure reality. Nanna spared me all the semi-realities that the wall was so good at conjuring. I wanted Nanna to see me as I was now, not my possibilities that lay hidden in the future. When she leapt into the "afterward," I saw her fleeing the here and now. I was afraid for myself, but I was even more afraid for her.

3 July 2014

My beloved Nasser,

I couldn't believe it when I got home yesterday, put on my pajamas, and jumped into bed. I turned on the computer and there was *Notting Hill*. If it weren't the month of Ramadan, I would have invited you to join me for a bowl of popcorn.

By the way, I forgot to include the picture of your dear friend Hamza with my last letter. I felt bad that I was not able to visit his grave the other day to tell him what I saw in your eyes when you looked at the picture of the two of you together. And when you asked me to have Shatha tell him how much you missed him, I was moved by your love for him.

I'm writing this at work. Stop looking at me like that, or you'll distract me!

Now it's 2:13 p.m., and I'm back home. I'm about to start the film. Should I make a place for you next to me? Come over, please, if it's not too much trouble!

It's 4:31 p.m. The movie's over. I'm not able to talk at the moment. I'll just say that you're the most beautiful thing that has ever happened to me. Indeed, you are more beautiful than anything I've ever imagined. I'm feeling too emotional to write. But I need to tell you how much I love you. I don't know if you anticipated what this movie would do to me, but it's taken me very far away indeed. I remember all the details of our first meeting. Sometimes, a feeling comes over me that I want to embrace everything inside you with all my strength. That I can stop time when I'm with you. That I can reassure you enough that you'll stop asking me to keep my distance and leave myself an escape hatch. Why can't you understand how happy I am to have finally found you? No matter how long the journey, you're by my side. I'm waiting for you. When will you realize, Nasser, that you're the person I've been waiting for since the day I was born? And that I cry every time I remember your request to make my escape? I need to be able to say your name without you being afraid, or you being afraid for me. My happiness with you is something I'll never find with anyone else. I've stopped searching, Nasser. I've arrived.

Love,
Nanna

* * *

Love is a remarkable thing. So is its ability to shorten long roads and to unite terrestrial worlds with celestial ones. It is a reconstruction, a bridge building, a greening of glassy deserts, devoid of water and dust. Love is a remarkable thing. The guide for believers and the shortest path to God. With love, colors dance across your melodies. Reconciliation and tolerance expand within you. You forgive the one who is wrong about you and the one who does you wrong. You plunge right in, without fear of drowning. You soar, and if you fall, you fall upward. The highest and lowest of God's creatures address you. The green unfolds, and deserts take two steps back. Your bonds and chains do not return. Love suspends the fears and anxieties within you. It compensates for everything you deny, for your walls, and for your falling after a long period of hanging.

When you love, all walls and ceilings inside you collapse. Your shadow falls, still standing. Your hands take possession of your bonds.

When you love, God descends to His lowest heaven. He places His hand upon yours and prays a final prayer for you.

When you love, you are your time, you are your place. Nothing limits you, nothing stands against you. There is nothing before you and nothing after.

When you love, you go to sleep exhausted, and you wake up jubilant. You are a king. Each night is a raid, and victory crowns your morning. You have a lover on every shore.

When you love, you are the tolerant peacemaker. You are the one who forgives, who loves, who drinks, who plunges in. You are the knight, and every sword is your sword.

When you love, you become a heretic. You are the outside, the inside. You are the Abbasid, the Umayyad, the Fatimid. You contain a tribe from every side.

When you love, you are the perfection of the city, the countryside, and the tent. You are the refugee, the exile, the one who swims or slips across the line. You return from your Nakba.

When you love, your voice returns to you. You give up counting your wounds, and even if you are healed, Nanna spins new wounds for you.

Nanna is in her white clothes, come once again to test the limits of my endurance. "White suits you," I once told her. So she wears white to punish my blushing face.

"Come closer, Nanna."

"Should I stand up?"

"Yes."

"Like this?"

"No, even closer."

"Nasser, I'm afraid. I don't think I can bear coming any closer."

"You said you weren't afraid when you're with me."

"I remember."

"Come closer, and don't believe the glass wall."

"I don't believe anything except you."

Nothing separated me from Nanna's face except our breaths, which the glass constrained until it began to sweat in embarrassment.

"Dear God, send prayers upon our master, Muhammad!"

"Stop it!"

"What's the matter, Nanna?"

"I'm more afraid."

We sank back into silence. Me, Nanna's face, and a transparent glass wall that did not believe us when we pretended it wasn't there. Here was Nanna's face, in all its bare elegance. Angels fell from their sky. They hung their clothes on the nearest cloud and came down to swim naked in Nanna's face.

My wall observed this new hanging of mine. It read the letters I wrote. It butted in whenever I read my letters from Nanna. After our meetings, it would ambush me with pictures or paintings to increase my fear for her. I never would have been able to resist my wall were it not for Nanna's growing resolve and her insistence upon joining my ordeal. I returned from each meeting with her stronger. My anxieties diminished, even as I grew more adept at ignoring the transparency of the walls and the details of life beyond them. Nanna was all I wanted. The world had already offered me the most beautiful thing it possessed, so nothing else could tempt me. My wall could read the situation, but it was stubborn, and not a day went by when it did not renew its attempts.

12 July 2014

My beloved,

With this letter, I'm sending the words of the song that you like from *Notting Hill*. Nasser, I believe that God loves me very much, for the man I love is like no other. My beloved is perfect at loving, but in his own unique dialect. It's clear he is copying no one. Indeed, I am certain that no one has mastered love the way he has. He enfolds me with his gaze. He persuades me with every word he utters. My Lord has created no other beloved for me upon this earth. One who loves me exactly as I would wish. He surpasses every scene of love that my imagination could invent. He rises above all my expectations and dreams. This man has become the engine of my life, even without his physical presence.

My God! What have I done to deserve this gift? I thank God every moment of the day that he has bestowed you upon me. I feel, Nasser, that the words of this song from the movie were written just for me. Every time I hear it, I'm overwhelmed by a sensation that you are addressing me and touching my soul, even as you turn me into contradictions: the weakest and the strongest creature upon the face of this earth.

Nanna

Around that time, my mother began distressing me anew with her questions. She came to every visit expecting to hear some news to ease her mind. Visits from the released souls reinforced my mother's questions. She blamed her Lord more and more for delaying my return. I grew tired of the repeated questions. "I'm here, Mazyouna, and I don't have any answers to ease the weight of your long nights. My journey is not yet over, Mother, and I can't bear your questions any longer."

Mazyouna wept, and my sisters joined her tears. I became harsh. "I'm not dead yet, Mother! My prison is no graveyard for you to come and wail over those dwelling here. Stop burying me here! Stop weeping at every visit. This is me. I'm still here! I haven't stopped loving you. Isn't this my chest, rising and falling? Count my breaths if you want!"

My mother was alarmed at my reaction, and so were my sisters. They tacitly decided to abandon their questions, or at least hide them somewhere I couldn't see. The visit resumed its old, comfortable pattern.

I told them about my deepening feelings for Nanna. The shock of the news drained all the color from their faces.

"My heart could feel it," said my mother. She had spoken to Nanna more than once, and she had many kind things to say about her.

"I love her, Mother."

"And I love her too," said Mazyouna.

Have You Ever Informed a Prisoner of His Mother's Death?

At seven in the evening on Wednesday, the third day of Ramadan in the year 2019, we received news from the Red Cross that the mother of a prisoner named Kamal had passed. The other souls wanted me to accompany them to Kamal's cell to break the terrible news. We waited for the call for the evening prayer in order to allow him to break his fast and ease his hunger and thirst. Then we entered his cell. An hour later, we were back.

Have you ever informed a prisoner of his mother's death? I have, and it wasn't the first time. After waiting for Kamal to finish his iftar, we entered his cell, feeling embarrassed and ashamed, much as the angels of death must have felt when they burst in upon his mother's bed. Kamal's mother had resisted her visitors. She slammed the door in their faces, yet they insisted. She asked for more time, just until her next visit to the prison. "Allow me one last Eid!" she said, looking into the angels' eyes. "Kamal has asked for some clothes, and I haven't had time to get them yet. Come back next month. Kamal hates it when I'm slow with his requests, and I couldn't bear to keep him waiting. Come back next month! On my last visit, I forgot to memorize all the changes etched upon his face by fourteen years of iron. Come back in a month. Let me express my love one last time. Give me time to pray that he'll only weep for me a short time." The angels of death covered her face and ended her life quickly, fearing that they might waver in their mission.

We entered Kamal's cell. We covered our faces so he would not see in them the funeral procession of his mother. We sat down without saying a word. Kamal finished washing the dishes. He sat beside me and asked about my health. The covered faces began to utter brief generalizations about the inevitability of death. Their talk became more specific and urged Kamal to be steadfast and strong. He looked at them in surprise as they went on speaking.

"Who was it?" Kamal asked me.

"Your mother," I replied, without any hesitation. Despite my embarrassment, I didn't cover my face. I didn't wait for another month or some future visit. Your clothes came too late, Kamal. There will be no Eid to end your long fast of iron.

Kamal covered his face, but not out of shame or embarrassment. He clutched the iron bars and buried his face between his hands. He cried until he choked on his sobs and his face wet the iron. We spoke to him about a merciful Lord who had taken his mother one hour ago. I don't think Kamal heard what we said.

"Mama!" Kamal kept crying out to his mother as he embraced his iron bars.

Have you ever informed a prisoner of his mother's death? I have, and it won't be the last time. Be gentle, O angel of death. I swear, you've taken nothing more dear to us than this...Be gentle, O angel of death! Come gently. Blessed be the one taking; blessed be the one taken.

But I still have my tale to tell. Where were we? Talking about Mazyouna, who rejoiced to learn of her son's beloved. Would my mother have rejoiced like that if one of her granddaughters expressed a desire to become engaged to a prisoner, someone already behind bars a quarter century, and on his way to a quarter century more, even harsher and longer?

The Body

I had abandoned my hanging upon the wall. That's what passion does: it transports us from one form of hanging to another, something completely different. It rewrites our past, rearranging all the letters, swapping some words for others. It answers the question marks we've put off for the future. It resurrects events long buried, even as it pushes to the margins other incidents we believed were central. Love rounds the corners of the squares within us. It throws us into the center of a Sufi circle. We lose our grip on the essence of our senses; their truth mixes with fantasy. We spin, uncertain if we are in motion or if we are the stable point around which everything else is spinning.

Love changes the way we address our Lord, even as it brings us closer to Him. It brings Him closer to us, unmediated by books, notebooks, and dubious verses of scripture. We hear our inner voices. We speak with other beings and hear their words. Branches bend down when we pass beneath them, and if there are no branches on the wall, we draw them there, together with leaves and fruit. We keep spinning in our Sufi circle until we realize we are part of everything around us. We harmonize with our music and our dancing. We correct our mistakes, even though we are no longer ashamed to make them. We seek an apology on behalf of others, if they are unable to do so, and offer forgiveness after every apology. We are pained when someone else waits for days, and we cry for those who despair and give up waiting. We invite to the table of our love every broken heart, and we bind up its wound until it heals or else it dies.

In prison, we souls have no use for our bodies. Bodies are nothing but a heavy burden, bound by laws of nature that limit our ability to spin, soar, and swim through the clouds around us. Bodies possess nothing more than hunger, thirst, and fatigue. They eat only in order to search for a lost appetite and old scents that might recall a time and place lost in memory. They drink, but nothing quenches their thirst. They grow tired from doing nothing. Bodies believe the ignorant chaos of the senses, with their stupid explanations about presence and absence. Bodies dance to any music, only to keep stumbling and losing the beat. They fall ill and recuperate in their narrow way, or they die without any illness we understand. Souls in prison go on this way, dispensing with their bodies. Both sides live in a state of mutually agreed separation. Bodies sink into their lower world while souls go on soaring, denying all the physical surroundings that oppose their spontaneity. Neither side holds the other back; there's no meddling and no objection except when necessary to guarantee a state of civil peace between the two worlds.

In prison, bodies lose their object and their goal. We take care of them only to ensure they won't burden the soul. What need have we souls for arms that cannot embrace, either in greeting or in parting? For hands that do not extend when we need them? For fingers that do not undo the buttons of a dress that hides untold secrets beneath? What need have we for lips that do not receive other burning lips? Or for legs and feet that have stopped carrying us toward an abducted future? Such bodies have sunk into illiteracy and ignorance, without language or discourse or meaning. They shudder under the spell of an unexpected nighttime passion, of which only a confused memory remains in the morning. Or they convulse to a waking fantasy, muffled and hidden away from the eyes of others. In prison, bodies become a meal for the walls, which are never satiated and come to feed upon us again. Bodies are transformed. They become an object both boring and pitiful. They grow up, get old, turn gray, and lose all desire to live. They remind us of our bonds, for nothing in us except our bodies accepts being chained.

"Nasser, I think I'm entirely you."

"I'm certainly a part of you."

"When will you come to rescue me?"

"From whom?"

"From you! From your absence and from your presence."

"Don't lock the door on your only way out, Nanna."

"By all that is holy, don't start on that again!"

"But I am the absence, and I am the presence."

"Why do my dreams frighten you?"

"Why does my reality frighten you?"

"Don't deny my fear and my anxiety."

"Run, Nanna! Get away while you still can."

"I swear I'll never run except toward you."

"Your stubbornness will kill me someday."

"Would you prefer to die any other way?"

"In that case, don't believe in this glass wall."

"I'll say it again: I don't believe in anything but you."

When we fall in love, our bodies return to us. Love resurrects bodies. That's what Nanna taught me. I believed it, and so did my body, which began rebelling against the way I ignored it, just as it resisted my soaring, which did not always get very far from the body's primary, animalistic functions. Yet I actively prevented my body from taking any part in Nanna and all her fullness. That kind of experience would be a fall into an abyss that lacked the necessary vocabulary to match the spirituality of our meetings.

During this time, I maintained my bias for the world of the sky. That was the discourse that prompted Nanna to take hold of the first thread of blood. I kept attempting to make Nanna believe in the worlds she was spinning. Neither of us would be able to escape if we became caught in a strictly bodily language, governed by a mass of concrete walls and some glass ones, that could not rise to the level of our souls' conversation. The language of earth people was limited to words that fought together, struggled, and killed—with or without justification. Words that encroached, drove out, and deceived after they explained away their betrayal. If I encountered any earth woman, I would never be able to declare that I loved her. Nanna, however, came from a different world, not this terrestrial one. She proved it by repeatedly returning to the wall, and by listening to the souls, their pains, and their strange talk coming from above, where they hung. She proved it, too, by her interest in universal cares that went beyond our own local concerns.

22 July 2014, 9:11 p.m.

Nasser, my fate…

I'm at the office. My work never ends! I quickly conjured you up before me, and the moments just before your arrival were the loveliest part of my entire day. I fear to mention things that I'm not yet ready to articulate. So let me just say that I've forgotten when and how I fell in love with you. It has started to seem that our connection has been going on forever.

One of your letters arrived. As soon as I began reading it, a strange feeling fluttered in my stomach. I cannot describe my reaction…Here were words written by your fingers. The box where I hide your letters has become my qibla, and I visit it every day. I promise you, Nasser, I will never surrender my love for you, not even if you remain in prison for an entire lifetime. Tonight your letter will sleep under my pillow.

Tomorrow, I will be in your home, the house that preserves your voice, your smell, and the fingertips of your soul. I will see the room that received your head when you lay down to sleep each night. I will pass through a front door that will soon open to receive you after a long absence. On that day, I will be there to receive you. Now I'll go to sleep, certain that you're on your way to me. You're getting nearer every day, and soon you'll pull me close and whisper in my ear: "Fear not! I'm with you till morning." I'll drive safe tomorrow, and I'll take the road across from the prison in case you might feel me going by!

25 July 2014

I'm back, writing again after a few days. My soul
has calmed down, and I'm finally able to share the
details of my visit to Aida Camp. The first thing I had
to do was pick out a gift for Mazyouna. Something
she said had stuck in my mind, which was that there
was no more patience in Aida Camp because she had
consumed it all. Since the Arabic word for patience,
sabr, is the same as the word for aloe, I decided to buy
her an aloe plant from a nursery nearby.

Your brother, Abd al-Fattah, met me at the
camp entrance, and when I saw him, I suddenly
went cold. I reached your house and met all the
members of your family. I had spoken with each of
them previously, but meeting them in person was an
entirely different thing. Mazyouna returned from
praying at the mosque, and I hurried over to kiss
her. She responded by calling upon God and saying
so many nice things, such as "O my dear, my life,
you have lit up the camp with your presence." I read
Mazyouna the letter you had written to her for Eid. It
made your sisters cry, but Mazyouna just took your
letter and kissed it.

Inside the house, the cold feeling returned. I
could almost smell you. How badly I wanted you to
be there with me! We entered your bedroom, and all
the tears I had been holding back poured out. This is
where you used to lie down and where you'd get up
each morning. I wonder who used to lie beside you on
that floor. Were there many of them, and did you love

them the way you love me? I'll tell you more when we meet soon.

Love,
Nanna

Nanna did not stop addressing my body. She did so in every possible way, and her ways were remarkable. She did it when she spoke and with the words she used. She did it with the clothes she wore. She did it when she grew her hair out because I asked her to, and also when she refused my repeated requests for her to tie her hair back to let me see her entire face. When she sat down, when she got up, when she objected to my interest in her face because it made me ignore what she was discussing. It was impossible for me to ignore her face and its aura, and I kept making new discoveries during the meetings in our little nook.

"Tie your hair back, Nanna."

"I don't want to."

"So stingy!"

"So greedy!"

"How dare you hide part of your face like that!"

"Don't tell me you've never seen one more beautiful."

"It's possible you're not the most beautiful of women, but I have no doubt that you are."

"These tricks of yours won't help you."

"Stop being so stingy and just pull back your hair."

"Fine, but I would need a hairpin."

"Improvise."

Nanna took a pen out of her notebook. She gathered her hair and bound it with the pen, revealing her whole face.

"My God!"

"Nasser!"

"I'd lay down my life for you, Nanna, body and soul."

"I'd lay down even more for you."

"If only the angels swimming in your face would leave, Nanna. I can't look at anything else."

"If only you would stay."

"Don't believe in my absence, Nanna."

"I want you with me."

"Believe me, I won't leave you, not even for an hour."

"Nasser, I want you with me. I need you!"

Nanna did not yet realize the degree to which she had brought my earthly body back to life, a body that had been controlled by the harsh physical laws of years, seasons, walls, iron, and glass. Nanna stripped away my body's absence and its marginalization. She turned it into an object of needing, longing, and waiting.

My body now had to respond to Nanna's questions and needs. I had to plant my chest everywhere that Nanna might lay her head. I had to stretch out a hand to clear a path for her, to join her steps along every road, to kiss her before she fell asleep (and after), and to address the ignited femininity of her flushed, rebellious body. Even as my body watched Nanna through the glass, it remained frozen in place, dead and unmoving. My body practiced its physicality, showing no mercy toward me or toward Nanna's appeals. It exercised its power through its weakness and its impotence. It turned into a monster by denying the young woman seated in front of it across the glass, pleading with it to come near.

I carried my exhausted body back to my cell. The guard escorting me watched my heavy, hesitating steps. He watched my body lose its balance and stumble along the short corridor that seemed longer than my very life. The transparent walls gave me no respite, for they didn't stop me from observing Nanna depart our little nook. I saw her get into her car and curse everybody nearby who interrupted her never-ending tears.

My body's functions gradually returned. Love causes our bodies to ignite, and we flee to our souls to be saved from a conflagration that is raging out of control. Nanna soon arrived and filled the room. She came to rescue me after seeing my need for her. Nanna became my ship when I set sail, and my wind when I wanted to soar. She was the shore where I anchored, and the dry land that cured my seasickness. A wall that shielded me from every anxiety. A ceiling where I could scrawl my thoughts. She was my sure path when I went astray and my whirling Sufi circle when the ground stopped spinning... Nanna became the answer when I was lost in my questions. She became my dwelling place when I was cast out.

10 August 2014

My love,

I miss you, I miss you, I miss you! A little while ago, I found a letter in my mailbox. How do you always manage to catch me at my weakest? Last night, I prevented the night from conjuring you up so that you would not see me like this. I cried so much, but I'm back now to clarify what I failed to explain earlier.

Before God, I vow that you are the only man who will ever dwell in my body, my heart, and my soul. I vow we'll name our future child after your friend Hamza. There will be no child like him, and from his name, people will know me as Umm Hamza. I vow to have no life except with you, and that I will maintain my vows, even if our journey lasts a thousand years. You are my life and my love. We will share, you and I, this white ceiling of mine. I vow to fear nothing when I'm with you, apart from any anxiety I might cause you. I love you so much, it hurts. I love all the contradictions of this love. Your existence has become my holy text; your love is my sacred law. Never have I felt such great faith, and all I ask from God is for some country to bring us together, someplace where I can find refuge and let myself fall asleep upon your chest. I will be your land so that you might become the plowman you formerly were.

I love you so much. I love Nasser the man, Nasser the person, and Nasser the mission. I sometimes imagine our first meeting, but without any glass barrier separating us. I'm unable to picture my reaction. Would I be content just to greet you and shake hands, or would I throw myself upon you, without the least care for custom and tradition? Do you ever think like that?

Two days ago, I went to the city of Tulkarm, and I picked out two silver rings for us. God help you,

Nasser, as you go from one captivity to another! Your
future life sentence awaits you, and I have no intention
of granting an early release, not even on the grounds of
good behavior.

Love,

Umm Hamza

How strange lovers are! If they are believers, then God, the
prophets, and the angels testify to their faith, and their belief
never fails. If they sleep, they have their own private mornings
to wake up to. If they are hungry, they do not eat. They curse
their own bodies and praise God for every hand that reaches
out, every arm that embraces, all lips that kiss, all feet that
walk, and every breast where the beloved lays their head. If
they pray, they finish early, they go long, they vary the words
of their invocations. If they die, they do not die, despite what
everyone believes.

I no longer saw anything through the wall except the
image of Nanna and the creatures surrounding her. My
body triumphed over my body as it cycled through different conditions. Everything that had fallen away hurried back
as though making up for lost time. My body believed the
worlds Nanna was spinning—and all the signs of her love.
My body devoted hours to cross-examining the hand Nanna
admired, the face she praised with a simple poem, the mouth
she sanctified with a kiss, the breast she dozed upon in the
middle of every night. Nanna did not spare any attentions
to my body—causing me to spend extra effort and longer
minutes in front of the mirror.

My body returned to me. With my body came the iron chains. I now collided with the wall every time I tried to soar without a good map of the surrounding physical world. I now faced the possibility of feebleness, old age, and the failure of exhausted limbs. With my body came my desires and my primary instincts, which had grown fractious after their slumber and demanded to be satisfied. Everything in my body began to scream Nanna's name. Here and now! All of my actions were for Nanna, and everything else was a waste of time and effort. I turned to Nanna whenever the walls bore down on me and my chains cut into my wrists. I wrote to her ceaselessly. Beyond the wall, there was no longer anything or anybody beside her. I halted wherever she did. Everywhere she trod I erected a tent for myself, and there I hung my clothes and my dreams, my desires and my passion for her to be near.

And now here was Nanna, taking oaths, vowing, and casting all her bread upon my waters. Crying and then crying some more, Nanna cried until I overflowed my banks, and my heavy body dragged me under. Nanna abandoned the ancient gods of Rome, and she searched for Canaanite gods that resembled her. She searched for the god El in the plains and the hills. She greeted Baal at Mount Carmel as he scattered fertility and plenty wherever he alighted. She abruptly turned to Baal's mother, Yam, creator of the universe, only to meet Ashira, Baal's wife, who was created from his rib. Nanna kept studying and searching, for she had not yet found the gods she had lost. Anat, the goddess of fertility, was busy arranging a hurried engagement, and Nanna had to wait. She waited a long time. She had waited an entire lifetime. She soared through the air. She sailed from one shore to another. She wandered through cities, reading the street signs. Nanna wanted to improve the world she was spinning without leaving anything to chance.

It wasn't easy, but I was finally able to put on the engagement ring that Nanna had bought. I kept it with me always, and I waited for Nanna to arrive. When she did, I hid the ring from the guard who came to get me. I hastened my steps, and the soldier made an effort to keep up. We arrived and the door opened. Nanna sat where she always did, a smile illuminating her face. I took the ring out of its hiding place and slid it onto my finger.

"I voluntarily accept my bonds, Nanna."

"Aren't you scared you'll regret it?"

"I regret my entire life before you."

"I think my love will be a burden."

"If only it were!"

"You make me sweeter and prettier, Nasser."

"You were always like that. Don't you believe what the mirror says?"

"Now I do, now that my mirror is you."

"Did you read what love engraved on the rings?"

"I read it."

"You are the end of my story, Nanna."

"And you are the beginning of mine."

So this is where lovers go, into an enchanted world. They bring their bodies, their souls, and their magic. This is where pilgrims come to meet their Lord, and no one in the city believes their account of what takes place. You don't care that the walls are transparent, for you have nothing to hide, and nothing to be hidden from you. Here, bodies and souls come together, with no incongruity or contradiction. Here, you are present in your entire being, with no existence apart from you. You join whichever of your earthly and heavenly companions you've chosen. What a world you have spun, Nanna!

14 August 2014

My beloved Nasser,

I can say with full conviction that I'm not angry your release has been deferred, and I know you won't accept any compromise that minimizes our people's victimization, even if it meant we might be together. At our last meeting, you said I tried to kiss you on the night of Eid. Such a bold move! I don't know if it's true! You also said that I was very good at kissing you, considering that it was my first kiss. Would you mind if I asked about your prior experiences? You are free to answer or refuse. I just want you to squeeze me against you with all the love you possess. Show my ribs no mercy!

22 August 2014

On this day, news reached me of the death of our poet Samih al-Qasim. At the same time, the bombardment of Gaza continues, with all its killing. So which thing am I crying for? Here are the final words that al-Qasim wrote on his death bed:

I do not love you, death, but neither do I fear.
You've taken my body for your bed, and my spirit as
your blanket.

But I see your shores are too narrow for me.
I do not love you, death, but neither do I fear.

Stay with me, Nasser. Never leave me. And don't ask me to go. You might be impossible, or you might be the fate decreed for me. Either way, I will be with you. You are my beginning, you are my end, and that's all there is. You might get the news at any moment that I've died from an overdose of love. Forgive me for being so discouraged and cross at our last meeting.

Nanna

Nanna believed what she was spinning, and she began to tell a story that resembled me. She narrated our meetings from a world to come. She conveyed what the fates decreed regarding her body and mine. Then she resumed hanging what she spun upon the gate of tomorrow, with all its possibilities. Nanna's spinning tested her fate and mine. She calculated her possibilities and my probabilities. Nanna did the same as any October girl: she changed, she varied, she went to extremes. She was not one to submit to fates other than those she herself wrote.

Nanna wrote to me often, and her letters filled my hours. She wrote her certainty, and she rejected any shadow of a doubt that wove its threads into my letters to her. My constant soaring annoyed her, as did my stubbornness every time she tried to bring us down to a terrestrial realm and a reality I never believed for a day. Nanna was my sole reality.

October

Nanna gave me back a virgin body, inexperienced in love and war. Falling in love is like a birth. It brings us back to the first line of the first writing. We do everything for the first time: our first cry, our first steps, and the first time we stumble and fall. Former knowledge no longer offers us anything. The body's memory is gone. A new process of learning begins, accompanied by complicated attempts to achieve a synthesis with the past. Aren't we all a product of our knowledge and our experiences? What was happening to my memory? And what about my body, which would grow tense in Nanna's presence, as though searching for some appropriate response? Her proximity made me tremble. I wished to kiss her, and it was as though I'd never kissed anyone before. My shaking fingers enraged me as I tried to unravel each of her riddles.

Nanna's sudden forays devastated me. A few loving words whispered in my ears, or a desire to do something wicked to my body, and I would be tongue-tied. She became expert at soaring, caring nothing for gravity or how the laws of physics applied to our nook. She was always a step or two ahead of me when I asked her to dance, and she would select the music.

Woe to my body! I'm not someone who fumbles over a kiss and loses his sense of direction. That's a secret knowledge I used to possess and often shared with others. I've never been someone who feels surprised or embarrassed in the presence of a woman, losing all my words. What was it that paralyzed my body's memory, which Nanna knew so much about? She learned about my previous life and my experiences before her. She learned about the transgressions and the regrets, about each wound and how it happened. She learned about women who did not master my body for long even though they left a deep trace. The memory of bodies is short, and their pains are poor, even when they strike deep.

"Did you love any of them? And I'm not talking about that girl in college who ignored you."

"No."

"But you…"

"Yes."

"How could you do that if you didn't love them?"

"It's not so hard."

"I see."

"It's a different alphabet, but we learned it well."

"Have you really mastered it?"

"Impressive diplomas and degrees are tattooed across my body."

"I don't think I want to hear any more."

"You can ask me anything you want."

"Do you want me to ask?"

"Would my answers break us apart?"

"No."

"I'm more of a virgin than you, Nanna, if that's what matters."

A contented smile came over Nanna's face, or at least that's how I interpreted it.

"What is it?" I asked.

"Nothing. I just like the idea that I'll be your first."

"And it strokes my vanity—or something more—that you will be my last."

How beautiful for a woman to pierce you to the core! A woman who intoxicates you after one glass, and who leaves you with no definable mood. A woman who comes to you regardless of your wishes, without asking permission or knocking before entering. She gives you no chance to get dressed, or arrange your stances, or prepare your reactions—and if you do, she strips them off and tears them up, making you organize everything from scratch. If you struggle to decipher her intentions, she swaps all the commas and periods and fills the page with question marks. An October woman in her capricious changeability, who expands a single orphaned hour into the four seasons of your year. She sets a time but does not appear; then she is there without warning. It's as though she comes to you saying:

I've come
I've come to you with secrets: be ready.
Shatter before me any mirror you want,
and scatter the dust of your being in the heart of a cloud.
Curse all the fates you want,

and expose your manhood at every female's door.
Ignore her surrendering pleas, and be not among the
　　merciful.

I've come to you like the sea: be naked.
Strip off your heavy jahili heritage, or whatever remains
　　of it.
Believe the words of heaven or don't.
Embrace all the beloved fables that Athens recounted,
or be a Spartan rebel whose sword edge slays every
　　border...
If you want, be what you want. I care not what others
　　have said about you.

I've come to you like a promise: you and I
are the children of October and November,
　　grandchildren of the iris, with leaves that refuse every
　　shadow of a fall;
two souls carried upon the breast of two promises.
White like a kamikaze who strives for death on your
　　breast, black like a night that waits
to pour your bitter morning coffee—
sweetened, if you want, with kisses.

I've come to you like a ghost: be a cloud.
Forgive all your women for what they left behind
on a body betrayed by its wounds.
Wounds that do not enjoy the blessing of forgetfulness.
Draw your wall closer, for place has no place in this
　　place.
Release all the seasons and years that came before me.

I've come to you with a scream: be stubborn.
The most beautiful of sounds is to scream "No!"
There is no god but the one dwelling in your face when
    you see me.
There is no prayer but the weeping of fingers.
At the gates of my secrets, be stubborn.
There is no chain but the one you believe in.
There is no glorification but the dying of your noes
and their slain sound upon my mouth.

I've come to you with forgiveness for all your sins, so
    banish prayer and fasting.
Don't trust in your good intentions,
for I am a woman of Eastern passions, of autumn moods,
and the intentions of my October upon your November
are, if you wish, very wicked indeed.

I've come to you like the sun: Do you see
the lines of light across my body, and the dark of the sea
in your absence and in my yearning?
Come as quick as you can!
The sun does not dwell in a body twice, and I am a
    thirty-year-old woman,
so keep your talking and your flirtation for some other
    time.

October:
The Beginning
of the Story...

October:
The Autumn of Waiting...

October:
The Eternal...

Alas for my body now because of Nanna! Where were all my bold claims and my wounds? Where were my women and my fantasies? The wounds and their causes have all vanished, as though they have healed or have died, and there is not even a scar to recall them. Where were my damp, sweaty evenings, and my stolen minutes in a dark, scarcely lit corner? I observed what Nanna's body was saying in its various languages—some I knew, others foreign to me. She was discovering her body through my actions and her reactions. She advanced when I pulled back, and she stopped me in my tracks if I moved too fast.

I was at a loss about what to do for Nanna's birthday. How would I give her a gift? What kind of gift is even appropriate for the woman who has given you your life, your body, and the letters of your new vocabulary? Who transforms your dizzy spinning into a Sufi dance that carries you upward? Who releases the reins of your walls and begins protecting you from their transparency, until she becomes your stable wall that restores your balance?

October 2014

To my love and the sweetest thing that ever happened to me:

My birthday is now over, and I can confirm it was one of the very best. Thank you for the gifts, and especially the embroidered dress. The bouquet of roses was delivered, and then I went to the post office and found your letter, which contained the card where you wrote, "With every birthday, may I be your love, and may you always be close enough to touch." How do you know me so perfectly? I cried so hard from a happiness deep enough to last a lifetime.

I see myself groping toward your breast. I'm late because I get lost in the details of your face for a while, but I always arrive and lie down in a safe place upon your chest. You are the lord of my life! If only everything about me, body and soul, were intertwined and wrapped around you! Here I am, rushing headlong, and I love how it feels to crash into you. Everything about you attracts me, and I cannot wait for the moment when our bodies meet for the first time. And now, enough of your tricks! Tell me about our first meeting to come—every last detail.

Love,
Nanna

Nanna's birthday presaged the arrival of October like an iris on the seashore. It watches the first breaking of the waves and does not turn to read the names of the ships or their destinations. The iris announces a yellow autumn that has not yet decided to fall but keeps hanging on until the final hour. Nanna proclaimed her October, and she made an appointment with my November... The sea, the shore, and the iris kept her company as she waited. She spun its arrival, coming slowly, deliberately, and she hung in her closet all the colors that come after yellow.

"It kills me every time you wear white."

"I can change, if you want me to."

"I'll be so angry if you do!"

"You're impossible."

"This white simply refuses to die."

"Would you really kill it?"

"No! I want to scatter it in every direction."

"And then?"

"It will come back to me as a poem."

"These aren't the dimensions I was considering."

"They're exactly the dimensions I can't do without."

"So greedy!"

"No! Just a coward who's afraid that he knows exactly what's coming."

"Just like you to slip away, to hide behind your excuses."

"Aren't you afraid of killing me? Of killing yourself?"

"Is there such a thing as killing in love, Nasser?"

"Yes, Nanna: in so many ways."

* * *

It became necessary for me to delve deeper into my body's memory, dislodging the soil with fingers and scooping it out by the palmful. I wasn't able to face Nanna's onslaught with a body that lacked even a single experience to help it understand this incandescent being that came with such youth and vigor. Nanna possessed every forbidden fruit. As they ripened, she prayed to her Lord for a harvest when the time was right. I examined my wounds and bruises thoroughly. Could I recover the memory of old kisses? Or the shadow of bodies who imposed their authority upon my young body, and the others that I approached, ready and willing?

I searched for something that would dislodge a virginity now more than two decades old. I sought help from every sensation I began to awaken out of a long, deep slumber. It wasn't easy. I began with short, slow steps. I revealed to Nanna some of the secrets of the nighttime liaisons I imagined for us. I wrote to her about our shared tomorrow, about the dreams I pleaded with God to grant. I amplified the carnal details of our assignations. I became more entangled. My body panted to keep up.

I remained afraid that if I spoke plainly, Nanna would not believe the truth of what took place during our trysts. I feared she would see them as the product of a capricious imagination, or else deferred promises, waiting to be fulfilled. Would Nanna believe the new signs on my body? Would she believe my halting breath? The red lipstick on my shirt? Her torn dress? It was not only my imagination, as testified by my pain when each assignation was over. Here were Nanna's eyes. Here was her mouth. This was where she hung her clothes.

My hand burned from the cool marble of her body. Her scent clung to my clothes and my naked skin.

My body was emerging from its shell. It came rough, without any refinement to help it cope with Nanna's early visits. The process required numerous evening assignations until its manhood was trained and disciplined. The intimate passages in my letters to Nanna increased. We met at different times and places. We conspired further against the souls in the cells when Nanna decided to arrive late one night in order to confirm some of the details of our last visit. Without any advance warning, she took her usual place upon my bed.

Nanna's repeated nighttime visits only provoked my wall's rage.

November 2014

Upon the birthday of the most precious beloved...

To my love, the one most precious to my heart. With every birthday, may you be my love. With every birthday, may I be your beloved. With every birthday, may you be my helper—my nasser—just as I will be yours. Nothing but divine providence arranged our meeting. How wonderful is heaven's care!

Today, it is I who will take you on a long date, so please wear something warm. The rain came out of nowhere and betrayed me when I celebrated my own birthday last month. But tomorrow it will make things up to me with sunshine. I will be me, and I will be you, and the Jaffa Sea will complete our trinity. I will thank the sea for its loyalty, and for granting my secret prayers when it gave me to you.

The sea isn't calm today. It's as rough as it ever gets, like someone expecting our arrival—or warning against it. Neither you nor the sea is aware of what will happen, and I think I can picture the surprise on your faces. But I'm going to withhold the details, just like you would do, for this is my night, mine, and this is my date, and I've chosen the place. Nothing will save you from a certain drowning when I swoop down upon you. Yes, this is me talking to you! Don't be surprised! Only you could have drawn such words and actions from me. What have you done to me, you, gift of the sea, you, my master in the world of the sky people! I'll lay your head upon my breast so you can hear my heart telling you all that it could not say before.

I hope, my life, that you will like my gift and also our date.

Love,
Nanna

My wall continued its quarrel with me. It offered no support and never lifted a finger except to accuse. My wall hated Nanna, and it hated her October. It hated her visits when she was late and when she came early. It hated the smells that clung to her—I think Nanna strove to accumulate those odors on purpose. It hated the articles of clothing I forgot on my bed. It hated our morning talks about her, and the ones in the evening too. The wall hated Nanna's continual spinning. It hated my complete preoccupation with her and how I missed her when she left early. I never revealed to Nanna my wall's hatred of her. I think I told her the exact opposite—I no longer remember. My wall hated Nanna's month that had just passed, and it began hating my month that had just begun.

My wall suddenly began talking to me.

"Since when do these months mean so much to you?"

"October, you mean, or November?"

"Stop being so clever. I know you too well for that."

"It seems that your question makes no sense."

"On the contrary! I know you and these wounds of yours. Am I the one who caused them?"

"Am I nothing but my wounds?"

"Are you anything else?"

"What about Nanna?"

"If your Nanna isn't another one of your wounds, why can I smell your pain?"

"I thought you had stopped addressing me and smelling me."

"Who said I was addressing you?"

"Whose voice is this, then?"

"Yours."

No mercy and no forgiveness. My wall no longer had either the one or the other. It was cruel and spared no means of punishing me ever since I had let it go. If only walls had memories like our bodies!

We wrote a lot, Nanna and I. We met, time and again, seated on both sides of the glass partition in our nook. Cello music played in the background, but there was nothing in the music that could keep me from hearing the sound of Nanna's crying, which accompanied each of our subsequent visits. Nanna believed and trusted that the goddess Anat had blessed our engagement. She saw how our land and sky flourished when the god Baal descended from high atop Mount Carmel and created an oasis for himself alongside our small nook. She believed and trusted, and she cried for her faith and her belief. Nanna cried so much that her tears became the companion of everything we said and did. Tears before us, and tears after us. She cried when we spoke words of love, and she cried when we stopped talking. Nanna just kept crying.

The Tears of the City

God alone has the right to be alone.

—TURKISH PROVERB

28 December 2014

Nasser...

The things you said in your last letter made my
world spin. You have finally abandoned your demure
tone. You made me so happy with everything you
described about our nighttime meetings, about a
tomorrow that will unite us, and about a beneficent
sky looking down upon us from above. God be with
you, Nasser! You've made me love my body even more.
You're not the only one who can live with these bonds
and this life sentence, so stop using them to keep me at
a distance. They've become part of my existence.

Every year, I make a list of the things I hope will
happen. This year, I've crossed most things off the list
because you've made them come true. All that remains
is for your chest to become my pillow, and for your
face to light up my mornings. Why did you suddenly
check yourself during our last nighttime encounter?
I need you to lose control sometimes. Your rushing
makes me dizzy. God! How you spin me round!

31 December 2014

The year is coming to an end. A year that gave you to me after I began to lose my faith in love. Ahlam Mostaghanemi was right when she said, "Love comes to us from a time and place we least expect." In 2015, I will love you more and more. But for now, forgive me! I have so much to do at the office. But don't worry! Your girl can work wonders ... I'll be back when I can.

3 January 2015

I cried a lot today. It's the anniversary of your arrest. I cried so much my parents were worried about me. I cry a lot these days, and often for no apparent reason. But the one thing I know is that I want you here with me. Upon my chest, in my eyes, above all my care and my pain. How can a person love another person so much? I don't know, but I do. I love you before the tears and after.

My God, how I love you!

Nanna

When our bodies suffer some wound, we let out a curse. When the wounds run deep, we curse our ability to be wounded and lose so much blood. We become angry when pain makes its home at the site of the wound. The pain begins making forays against uninjured limbs, yet we refuse to acknowledge that any one part of us can disrupt the rest of us. Why should a limb fail if our chest is struck? Why does our chest heave faster if a leg twists beneath us? Our spirits are oppressed by the body's false claims. The body projects frailty to weigh down souls that soar through the air. In turn, our souls curse our bodies, listening to laments they cannot believe.

Wounds of the spirit, however, are complete and universal, both in the strike and in the bleeding. The incapacity they bring is absolute. Wounds of the spirit remain: they do not move on or grant us time to restore our strength. They set their roots deep within us, as though they've been there from the very beginning. We begin describing ourselves as a wound, and nothing but another wound awaits us. This wound makes no sound: no scream and no curses to absorb all our anger and frustration. Our bodily reactions are frozen, insulated from wounds that strike the soul. Our souls find themselves squeezed inside our bodies. When they find no way to escape to a wider space to plant their pains, our souls feel even more trapped, and so we cry.

"Why are you crying?"

"I don't know."

"I think I do."

"Please don't say anything."

"Nanna, I'm right here."

"Nasser, stop trying to cure my tears."

"But when will you stop punishing me with them?"

"I'm not weak. I'm not a coward. Don't be afraid for me."

"Love is not a test of our strength, Nanna."

"I just want to be with you. How can you call that weakness?"

"When will you believe?"

"Believe what?"

"The power of the worlds you spin."

* * *

It's said that our bodies take refuge in tears when they can no longer endure the pain. But I don't believe it. I don't credit our bodies with a spiritual act like crying. That's what crying is: a spiritual act, silent, deep, and questioning. When wounded deeply, souls are embarrassed to scream and curse or react in some other bodily manner. All they need is a solitary corner to receive their flowing tears. A distant corner that asks no questions and is unconcerned about the reasons. It doesn't care if the soul heals or if it dies. A cold corner, which doesn't resist when wounded souls crouch there for a long, wet hour.

"Nasser, I . . ."

"You are the world you spin, Nanna. Here is my blood, and here are its threads."

"Each time I leave this nook of ours, it's as though my soul is departing me. I'm choking and afraid."

"I return to my cell and I find you on my bed. You've hung your clothes across what was once my wall."

"People tell me to pull back now, before I become even more involved. I'm choking and afraid."

"My wall has abandoned me. It said I betrayed it when I let go. It blames me constantly."

"People don't believe you are possible. They confuse me by talking about what's likely to happen to you."

"My wall hates that you have become my only possibility."

"Hold me closer!"

"Can't you see that I already am?"

4 April 2015

To Nasser, Nanna's soul:

I've heard a lot about souls having a second half. I've always liked that idea, but I'm only beginning to understand it now. I always wanted a man with presence, and now I've gone and fallen in love with a man who is powerfully present, even when he is absent. Yet you want me to run away from you, Nasser? The only time I fled from you, I leapt into your arms. Just let me go further and deeper, my other half! Beyond the suffocation, beyond the drowning, who knows what you and I will discover.

I know, my dear, that I caused you much anxiety when I lost my grip and cried. I'm sorry! I felt very close, but at the same time, so far away. When I was leaving our little nook, I felt I was returning to a world that didn't understand me. Being apart from you is so painful, Nasser. Why do I have to be torn away from you each time? I only live during the hours I spend with you. These are tears of love. You have to believe me! I only want to be surrounded by you. Oh, if only you knew!

18 April 2015

I hate this month. If only it would end! The nighttime tears have come back to stake a claim on my bed…I cry so much. All I wish is to find you embracing my head and telling me that it will all be over soon and that we'll be together.

Love,
Nanna

Nanna cried for the months that lay before our feet. Nanna cried for the glass wall of our nook. She cried for the pages of our letters. She cried when she wrote, and she cried when she read. The more we spoke about love, the more she cried. We'd flee to other topics, but when we came back to love, Nanna would start crying once again. Nanna fought against her tears. She fought even harder when I pointed to the escape hatch.

"Nanna, I want you to promise me something."

"Anything you want and more."

"Promise me, Nanna."

"I promise!"

"If your feelings for me lessen, even a little, come and tell me."

"Why would you say that?"

"Because I won't accept it, Nanna."

"Won't accept what?"

"Half feelings."

"I know my tears betray my weakness. But you're the only one I can disrobe my weakness in front of and reveal it without shame."

"I don't want this love to transform into a monster that threatens your sense of balance and keeps reducing you to tears when we meet. I don't want you to cry."

"What monster, Nasser? I'm fleeing monsters when I come to you."

"But I can't take all this crying."

"I'll stop."

"Okay, but will the tears?"

"You're scaring me, Nasser."

"Run away, Nanna! Run back to your little monsters."

"You once promised me that between us there would never be any one-sided decisions, that we would decide our fate together."

"Run away now!"

"I didn't think you'd go back on your promise."

"Nanna, if you ever breathe without me, if you ever feel entirely present in my absence, if you lay your head down, even once, far from my breast, come and tell me."

"I promise."

I addressed Nanna's fear with all the languages I knew. I saw her fleeing her fear—even looking down on it and calling it names—at least, that's what she did whenever she was with me. She didn't reveal how it tormented her hours and distorted all the plans she spun. Nanna, who yesterday could speak only of love in a way I never grew tired of hearing, was now drowning in her tears after fear came to fill the vast spaces of her universe.

Nanna tried hard to conceal her fear, but it was always there. It dominated all our meetings and letters. Nanna cried between the lines and in the margins. Fear dwelt on both sides of our glass wall. It beat me to the small gap in the glass if I moved to kiss her. With tears in her eyes, Nanna presented her longing, her loneliness, and her waiting. We'd wait until the tears dozed off, or else turned their attention elsewhere, so we could examine our feelings free from their intimidation. We wouldn't make any sound that might remind the tears we were there. We whispered, we gestured, we spoke with our eyes.

Tears crowded every open space in the room. If we were too slow, the tears arrived before us, put on their black abaya, and took up as much space as possible. They filled the sky with clouds that promised a heavy downpour. Tears set our table and began eating our bread before us, stealing the sugar from our kisses. In only a minute, they ruined the makeup Nanna had spent an hour applying. The tears changed the aspect of our nook, just as they changed our faces. The cello player now dressed in black to better suit the occasion. When Nanna cried, we no longer had any good news to cheer us up. Tears are the soul bleeding, and I had to sit there and watch it bleed. I cursed my nook, which had closed in upon Nanna until she choked. I went on cursing my nook until the moment came when everything stopped, even my curses. Then I was the one who cried.

Between our tears and our furtive talk about love, between dozens of letters and many meetings in our little nook, Nanna decided, after seeking my advice, to take a new job that required her to move to one of the neighborhoods of occupied Jerusalem.

"I'll find myself more in this new job."

"I'm happy for you, Nanna."

"But there's something else, and I don't want you to be upset."

"What is it?"

"I might not be able to see you more than once a month."

"That doesn't bother me. For you not to find yourself in your work would upset me more."

"Do you really mean that?"

"Are you really asking?"

"I knew you would understand, but I felt I had to ask."

"There is no such thing as time and place in the language of the people of the sky, Nanna. Just me and you."

"In every time and place, right?"

"Exactly."

"I'm very excited. It's Jerusalem!"

"A city looking out over a city, that's how you'll be there."

"I love you so much, Nasser."

"And if only my love and I were enough for you, Nanna!"

"That would be possible if you loved me like you love it."

"Love what?"

"Your Jerusalem. Your city."

Previously, I had found various ways of managing my mother's unending waiting. Out of kindness to me, my mother tamed her impatience, until, despite herself, she became an expert in the art of waiting and employed various tricks against it, against me, and against herself. I had to relearn all that with Nanna. Nanna's waiting moved through various forms, complicated and intricate, and nothing in my earlier dealings with my mother prepared me for the pain I felt. Nanna saw in me the prologue to her journey, while in her, I saw the culmination of mine. If she thought she had arrived, she simply confused the meanings of the word.

When we arrive, we hammer nails into the finish line in order to hang our questions, our wishes, and our desires. When we arrive, inspiration ends. When we arrive, we dump out the clothes, letters, photo albums, and memories from our journey, and we arrange them on the walls and ceiling. We tear up our passports, for we no longer care about borders or bridges. The train no longer stops at our station; we are no longer there. Now it only gives a short blast on its whistle when it passes in case we wish to send a prayer for its passengers to arrive safely at their destination.

How beautiful it is to arrive! To bid a final farewell to our waiting, without adding a wish for some future meeting, and skipping even a final cup of coffee to recall old times. How beautiful to arrive, when that arrival bears no signs of expiring. An arrival that brings a unique, singular, and matchless "I," the sole and final "I," and no other version. The "I" of contentment, acceptance, and surrender. An "I" ready to receive another "I," equally unique and complete, that comes to seek the "I" that will be its partner in arriving.

Nanna continued her waiting and her crying, while I remained in my state of arrival. I wrote to her about my own waiting, and how I had spoken my final words to it, helped carry its bags, and left it behind one summer under a tree with meager shade.

6 July 2015, 6:05 p.m.

Greetings, my love, my life!

This is the first letter I've written from my room in Jerusalem. Yesterday, Sunday, was the first day of my new job. My colleagues gave me a very warm welcome. At first, I was afraid of coming here. I quickly realized I was being overly nervous. It's much closer to Bethlehem from here... Your letter reached me, containing the poem I was waiting for. How can I convey my feelings to you? Now, after reading it, how do I repudiate my claim that Darwish's poem, "Wait for Her," is the most beautiful poem ever written about love? Your poem is the most incredible thing I've ever read. But did I have to wait all this time to discover that the most beautiful thing written about love would be written to me? How am I not the luckiest person in the world when I have become your poem? You are my beloved, you are all I wish for and want... Oh, how I love you!

28 July 2015

You also wrote: "You wear a robe made of clouds. Prophets write the marriage contract, with angels looking on. Hamza, my friend who was killed, leads you down the aisle to me, together with a whole host of witnesses." That is what I was needing to hear. I cried a lot yesterday, but today I'm better than ever. Thank you, my love.

In my new job, I'm learning more about the people's suffering on account of the Occupation. I know you're proud of what I do, but I promise, I'll work even harder to deserve your confidence in me. I'd rather die than stand powerless, and here is death, surrounding us on all sides and pressing in upon us. All our actions are paralyzed by a sense of impotence. But you and I will triumph over all. That is my promise. That is my religion. Thank you for making this move easy, for not making me feel like it cost you too much. Thank you for being my companion in my solitude, when it returned to live near me. This city

fills us with a strange feeling... I wish I could explain it
so I could capture it in this letter.

Nanna (in Jerusalem, loving you and
waiting for you)

Every woman is a city, with a history both recent and remote.
She has victories and defeats, and the names of founders,
conquerors, and all those who arrive with diverse intentions
and no invitation. She has her lovers, those who want her,
and poets who write about her. She has her poetry and her
prose. She has stones that preserve ancient memories. She has
streets that still echo with the voices of those who passed that
way. She has alleys that witnessed the stolen kisses of young
love. She has her gates and her keys, which she delivers only to
those she has come to trust. She has secrets, buried deep. She
bears the traces of those who despaired after her high walls
patiently rebuffed their fumbling attempts. She also has others, into whose beds she fell when they planted their triumphant flags upon her body.

Every woman is a city. We enter her, and our first impressions determine whether we return for a second visit. If this
city provokes our curiosity... If she has something to offer
beyond sidewalk displays, bars, and bookstore shelves... If
her waters accept our naked swimming with no disapprov-
ing looks... If she doesn't move away when we shamelessly
flirt... If she listens without interrupting, and without stealing a surreptitious glance at her watch... If she falls in love
with us without any consideration for our age or how long

we might dwell within her... If she daubs our clothes with a hint of her perfume... Then we return for a second and a third visit. We fall in love with her, and we dwell upon one of her balconies that looks out upon us.

Every woman is a city, and every man has a city where he lives, either in its heart or its outskirts. In her perfection, Nanna became a city. She became my village. She became the camp.

"Everything in the city flirts with me, Nasser!"

"Am I supposed to be jealous?"

"Maybe!"

"Of its stones or its holiness, or what?"

"Its men."

"Oh, its men?"

"You say it as if you didn't care."

"On the contrary, I care very much."

"How exactly?"

"I want them all to flirt with you."

"And then?"

"And then I'm the one that you flirt with."

"You bastard!"

"You got me!"

"Will you come to me tonight? Should I wait for you?"

"I'll come if you invite me, and if you only believe that I'm there."

"I believe, though I wish you'd come and stay."

"Fine, then I'll come, but you must not cry."

"I can't promise you that."

How strange is this Jerusalem of ours! So many have died for her sake, leaving behind their children, their wives, and their betrayals. They came from beyond the sun, riding upon the moon and the stars. One comes to settle, another comes to conquer, and a third is there with a mandate. They enter without asking the people if they need refining, conquering, or a mandate. They just enter, with no consideration for the cultures, societies, or religions of the ancient neighborhoods.

They pursue her in every possible way. The settler starts by flirting and offering small gifts that won't strain his wallet. He speaks some words of love that he doesn't mean in the least. He removes her clothes slowly and gently. He completes his business. Then he prays to his Lord with many long prayers of forgiveness that he doesn't mean in the least. He lets her dress quickly so that he won't be late to his prayers.

The conqueror dispenses with preliminaries. He proffers no flirtation, for she is ignorant of his alphabet. He offers no gifts, however modest, but saves them for another who might be more beautiful. He's in a hurry. He cares nothing about her clothes, which she took so long to embroider, but tears them away and callously gropes her chest. He mounts her like an animal. As his moans increase, her silence provokes him, and he becomes even rougher, seeking a cry that will restore his sense of virility. He completes his business. The city weeps, and he takes her tears as compensation for the cry that never came.

The one with a mandate comes hesitantly. He doesn't know if he should introduce himself with a gift, or with a short speech about love. Should he flirt with her, or would she spurn his flirtation as an impudence? He steps forward. He steps back. He sits beside her. Watching her reaction, he reaches out to touch her right breast. The lack of any expression on her face encourages him, so he kisses her mouth before breaking off quickly. He extends his other hand, probing deeper. No change. He cannot read her or understand her, and his patience runs out. Like males always do, he begins to remove her clothes slowly. She helps him, shortening the moment by a minute, or half a minute. He completes his business. He puts his clothes back on, neglecting certain details, for he suddenly remembers that he has left his children at home without anyone to watch over them.

They all died. Some of their tombs still exist, bearing names, years, and the circumstances of their death. Such memorials never fail to aggrandize the insignificance of their acts and deeds. Others have left behind nothing to mark their graves. All we find is a passing reference in books of dubious authority. They all died: those who flirted, those who were rough, and those who hesitated. When they are gone, she is left behind to pick up her clothes. She stops crying, heals from the wounds they planted upon her body, and quickly forgets them. She goes to sleep and wakes to new possibilities. She prepares her breakfast alone, and she prays for another attempt to come, something worth postponing breakfast for an hour.

It Was No Ordinary Day

Friday, 28 August 2015

Hi. I read what you wrote: "This is what our lives
will be like when my prayers come true." Reading that,
I hated you, I hated myself, and I hated your letters.
That's all you have to say after we've been separated
from our nook for nearly forty days? Am I now the
only one stupidly clinging to our faith that we will be
together soon and achieve our union? Why do you
doubt the single thing I believe?

I try to understand your reluctance to speak
about our future together, to understand your fear of
disappointments and setbacks. But that only makes
me feel lonelier than I've ever felt before. I can bear
anything except the idea that we won't be together. I
want you, despite this whole world, even if it plunges
us into a war of attrition... We meet tomorrow, and I
don't know where my mind will be when I come.

Nanna

5 September 2015

Greetings, my life...

I was sick to my stomach when the soldier opened
your door. It was as though I were about to see you
for the very first time. That visit won your pardon
for the sins of your last letter. You looked at me like
you always did, but this time things were different.
God has given you to me as a compensation for
all the wishes He ever denied me... I left our nook
with a desire to embrace the universe and some of
its creatures. Thank you, my love. I'm sorry for my
letter last week, and then for how I cried during
our meeting. When you looked at me, each of your
movements felt like a kind of threat. I've never felt so
confused with you before. How can time and place
contain such meaning? And bodies too? Confusion
never touches my body without leaving a scar. I
only have to return to that spot to relive the same
confusion, as many times as I want. I'm astonished
by your incredible ability to overwhelm me no matter
what distance lies between us.

Love,
Nanna

October 2015 arrived with a morning that seemed at first very
ordinary, just like the morning that preceded it and like the
one that would follow. I opened my eyes, and Nanna was the
first thing I saw. Her appearance shows how late we had stayed

up. First I nuzzle her face the way she likes. Then I turn to the rest of her body to make sure that nowhere hurts too much. I apologize—without really meaning it—to any places that hurt if I got carried away in my desire. I stand a brief moment in front of the mirror, removing any lipstick left behind by Nanna: I cannot risk drawing the attention of nearby souls to any suspicious mark, for I could not bear the glances, and possibly intrusive questions, that would follow. Nanna takes her time and, as usual, does not hurry to get dressed or wash her face. Besides the wall and me, there's no one who is slain by the beauty of this morning scene. No one else sees it. Nanna is extremely calm, even as she harasses my wall by prolonging her visit, seeing as she's incapable of starting her morning without a cup of coffee to wake her up. I start to make the coffee while Nanna puts on her clothes. The scene is no less deadly than before. She speaks, and no one but the wall and I hear.

"Bitter coffee... Tastes like you!"

"Is coffee any good if it isn't bitter?"

"A little sugar wouldn't kill you."

"I thought we agreed about this."

"Maybe I need you to remind me."

"We said we'd sweeten it with kisses."

"Did we really say that?"

"I know perfectly well you remember."

"Is that an invitation then?"

"If you want it to be."

"Strange, this thing you have with your coffee!"

"Is that a no?"

"On the contrary: a big, long, enormous, and exhausted yes."

"And sweet."

"Bitter too."

Coffee, with its sharp immoderation, has a mood that resembles the East. It accepts no half measures. If it wants to be bitter, it's not content for us to adopt some neutral position that eludes its bitterness. We may curse our neutrality when we discover, only too late, the sweetness we missed in its flavor. Coffee entangles us like a game of Russian roulette: we don't know what awaits us with our first sip, nor what comes after. Anything can happen, anything at all.

Before coffee, we are able to define our mood. We know where we stand, we recognize our morning reflection in the mirror, and we know the names of the souls and the inanimate objects around us. We can also distinguish our own faces without losing them even in a crowd of other faces. Before coffee, we feel certain about our senses and our sentiments.

But coffee ensnares you in its mood. It catapults you out of your current time and place into a dimension beyond time and place. It alters your judgments about the morning. It alters your appearance and sends you back to the mirror, where it might increase or reduce your satisfaction and confidence. Coffee has a clear position with respect to you, your questions, and your views. Don't believe its initial aroma. Wait for surprises that you don't expect after your first taste. Be careful of getting addicted if you are a person who likes routines, for you won't find coffee to be a routine that saves you. Or if you have a weak heart, for its bitterness represents a deadly risk. Or if you are a prisoner, for your day will no longer begin without a coffee to wake you up.

Our second October came quickly. It arrived just yesterday. Again, it made Nanna preface with tears whatever we
said or wrote. Her crying was hard; so was my impotence. I
opened a door for her to escape. She grew angry and cried
tears of fury. I offered a thousand apologies for my inability to
do anything. Nanna forgave me and refused my apologies. I
apologized for October, but she began blessing it and embracing me, and so I wrote a poem about the month.

October, you...

October came: don't close the prison door in its face.
    October
is the clouds bleeding. October is a breast that drips
with appointments and desires.

October returned, so wash away the tribal dust and
    ancient authority
of the Quraysh. October is lord of divine messages.
    October
is stories and tales.

October is the Ten Commandments and the lovers'
    ladder to heaven.
October is the breaking of bread and a prison visit
that happens again and again.

October is my beloved's face and her hair, twisted across
    my shoulder. October
is the weeping of those who part forever... Is it true that
butterflies weep?

October is the life of my beloved: twenty kisses, and
 another eight.
October is my alphabet when I draw her mouth
without any words.

October is a robe sewn by my mother, the sea's garb, the
 shore's
panting, and the burning grains of sand in
stolen glances.

October is for watering the earth and the seeds of
 passion within us. October
is the joy of a grandfather whose wrinkles and songs
are figs that ripen on his face.

October is a cup and Nanna, while I stand at the chasm.
 October
is the gown of a cloud, alone in the sky, swimming
 naked
in the evening shadows.

October is the black stone of my circumambulation.
 October,
the supple dancing of pilgrims between the hills of Safa
 and Marwa. October
is the very last miracle.

October is a postman who sleeps in his dream. October
 surpasses your dawn.
October says, "I am a servant, and I am your lord, and I
am the author of the messages."

October is a child's smile enshrined in a photo on my
    wall, lighting
up my day. There is no need for sun amid
a frenzy of kisses.

October is choking on the perfume of her handkerchief.
    October is the weight of prison
on my chest when I breathe. October is our flight when
    night falls
to become partners with the stars.

October, stay! After you, I have no life; and no life in my
    life
before you... October, speak of her and of me. October,
your silence bears no sound.

October is my beloved's question about past lovers. Will
    October
intercede for me so I die at the borders of her face,
the most coveted of graves?

It's Nanna's birthday. Our little nook is ready, and I'm waiting
for her arrival. I brought with me the poem I wrote so that I
could whisper it to Nanna. The cello player surprised me with
optimistic music today, though she came wearing black again,
so I guess it's a cautious optimism. Nanna arrived. She was
dressed in something new that accentuated all her charms.
Nanna is able to turn every dress she wears into a story. Yet
she remained prettier than anything she wore, prettier than
any story she ever told.

"Happy birthday!"

"Thank you, my love."

"It's a new year, Nanna."

"Then why do I feel so old?"

"Do the years still frighten you?"

"Very much!"

"We're only as old as we feel, Nanna."

"That's no consolation."

"Then what would be?"

"For you to get out of this place."

I took out the poem I had carefully hidden from my guard, from Nanna, and from the cellist in the black dress. I lifted it to my eyes and began reciting it to Nanna, who was taken aback. I read a line, maybe more. Maybe even half the poem. I no longer remember. When I raised my eyes to look at Nanna, she was gone. Nanna had collapsed off her chair.

Nanna fell far beyond the reach of my hands and my fingers. She fell into an abyss that went beyond the capacity of my earthly body, about whose union she had spun so much. How could any wound injure a soul so deeply? To make it fall from its lofty heights, from its ceiling, from its walls?

I recovered from my shock and saw Nanna drowning in an ocean of tears. I had never seen Nanna cry like this. Her crying had a sound that destroyed every living being within earshot. I could see nothing of her face but her tears. My hands dropped the page. "October" fell, yellow and fluttering, like the leaves of a tree that feel no pity for us when they fall and die. Every sound fell silent; even the cello music stopped. Nanna's tears covered that space, filled that moment in time. She tried to check them—out of kindness to me, I thought. But nothing could restrain her tears. They welled up and overflowed her eyes until no dry ground remained for us to stand upon in our nook. Her eyes cried. Her entire face cried. Her chest, the place I would lay my head, also cried. Nanna cried with every part of her body. Nanna was a miracle even in her weeping.

I suddenly stood up. I began circling our nook, which had closed in upon me. I strode in every direction. I buried my face in my hands. My hands fell from the walls, and I walked without direction. I heard Nanna scream, calling my name amid her tears, but I didn't respond. She screamed again, louder. Again, I buried my face in my hands, deep and wet. Nanna stopped screaming and began banging on the glass wall between us. She screamed my name again.

I found my voice. "Everything must end, right here and now."

"Nothing will end!"

"I can no longer bear how I'm torturing you!"

"I'm okay now."

"This narrow room will be your death, Nanna."

"I'll die if you let me go, Nasser."

"You'll leave this place now, and you won't come back. That's what you'll do."

"I won't."

"Look at yourself. Look at me. Is this what you want?"

"There's nothing else I want!"

"These are my bonds, Nanna. This is my life sentence. This is my hand that is incapable of wiping the tears from your face."

"I don't need you to do it. It was only a moment, and now it's passed. I just needed that fall."

* * *

Returning from that meeting with Nanna, I groped my way back to my cell. As I crept along, the walls emitted strange, frightening sounds and drew together until they were almost touching. The air I breathed caught in my lungs. My chains were so hot they glowed. The soldier escorting me transformed into a firing squad, rifles aimed at my chest, but if they pulled the trigger, they would have killed a man already dead. The path to my cell was interminable. I dragged my body along like someone dragging his own corpse, newly slain.

Back in my cell, Nanna was visible behind each one of the constricting, transparent walls. Behind the first, she cried without ceasing. She cursed my absence, not believing my lies about being with her. One moment, she spun a story about her future and mine. The next, she sat on her bed, found nothing to write about, and threw crumpled-up pages across the room. Beyond the opposite wall, Nanna added important, previously neglected details to her spinning. Nanna lived behind each of the walls around me. They displayed her image, in color and larger than life. I saw Nanna alone, and I saw her loneliness. I saw her defending our relationship against her friends' questions. I saw her flee to her room when one of her friends described the recent date she went on. I saw her flee from another friend who recounted her pregnancy, giving birth, and all the postpartum troubles. I saw her hiding me from her father, telling lies when his questions made her uncomfortable.

I saw the weak Nanna, and I saw the strong one. But her loneliness was too much to bear. I screamed into the heart of her isolation. Leaping from my window, I soared high above the soldiers' rifles. I traveled far, winding my way through villages that had once been ours. I swam through a holy night, soft despite the harsh conditions. Nanna's neighborhood was still awake, and her neighbors asked who the thief outside might be. I stood in front of her house for a while. Then I was at her door. I knocked so hard I thought my knuckles must make her door bleed. But Nanna didn't hear. Abandoning my religion and my morals, I entered the house without being invited. Then I was in her room, standing in front of her bed. I sat on one side of the bed and screamed, "Nanna! I'm here!" Nanna didn't see me. She didn't hear. Nanna went on not hearing or seeing me, and I kept sneaking out of my prison every night in case Nanna might finally believe I was there with her.

31 October 2015

It was a wonderful visit. Despite everything. I loved it very much, and I loved you even more. I loved myself when I saw the dress, your gift to me...I want you to understand why I collapsed, and I don't want my tears to do that to you ever again. If only you could have seen yourself, Nasser! I never imagined I would see you like that. I know it was hard on you, and that just proves how lucky I am to have you. I'm not weak, Nasser. No, I'm very strong. But I'm still a human who feels pain and suffers. Weak one moment and strong the next. None of my acquaintances can wrap their mind around what has brought us together. Talking with them is a waste of time now. Sometimes, I just

need to collapse and cry in front of someone who
won't barrage me with questions of why, and how, and
how long. But there's no one. So I come to you, and I
collapse with you... You say I need a shoulder to lean
upon. Yes, that's exactly what I need! But yours is the
only one I can find. So don't be unjust by proposing
some other solution. I want you to make room for my
weakness. Let me express myself fully, without the
need to hide anything. All I ask, Nasser, is that you
don't look for solutions. The only solution is for you to
come out of prison and for us to get better at waiting.

Be with me tonight!
Nanna

My fear for Nanna swept over me. I was not accustomed to
this kind of fear, which went beyond all past experience. A
fear full of questions and suspicions. A fear that punished
without mercy or compassion. A fear that ambushed me at the
door every morning with questions it spent the whole night
preparing. It begins with the most cruel: What are you doing
here? This is a fear that wastes no time. It seeks to kill quickly.
What am I doing here? I parted from fear a quarter century
before, when I departed this world, and in all that time, nothing occurred to bring it back. What am I doing here, when
Nanna is there, needing me and crying out in her pain at my
absence? What am I doing here? I do not belong in this confined sphere. These are not my walls. So what is all this clinging about? Is this ceiling for me? What has it done with all my

drawings? Why does it close in upon me? What am I doing here with all this iron on my body? What made my room so narrow, as though it were a prison cell? Why is the door locked and barred? What are all these other bodies doing here?

I'm there, helping Nanna prepare our breakfast after we've drunk our coffee, which is sweetened in our own special way. I'm there with Nanna, eating our breakfast as we make our plans for the day. That's what Nanna needs. That's what she is asking of me. I promised to be ready to do anything that would help her. Nanna wants me to kiss her, both before she sleeps and after, and I'll do it. She wants me to help her carry our daughter Salma to bed and to wake her up in the morning, and I'll do it. So what am I doing here? Why have I begun to believe in the length of my years, the solidity of my bonds, and the full length of a life sentence?

"Are you okay?"

"Don't I look like it?"

"Stop answering my questions with a question."

"I'm fine, and I love you more every day."

"Nasser, we're okay, aren't we?"

"You are the center of this existence. All my planets and I circle around you. So you decide how we are."

"I'm fine now and in a safe, secure place. I don't want you to be worried about me."

"I would die if anything happened to you, Nanna."

"And I have no life except with you. You are all I need, and without you, nothing is enough."

O My Wall!

The free man is free in every instance.
If some calamity befalls him, he is able to bear it;
if hardships beat him down, he does not break;
nor if he is broken and defeated, and ease has been
exchanged for torment...

—IMAM JA'FAR AL-SADIQ (D. 765 CE)

The questions became more insistent every day. There was nowhere I could escape my fears. It's a terrible thing for fear to be circular, with no private, sheltered corners for you to crouch and catch your breath. The circle of my fear narrowed a little more after each visit that put me in direct contact with Nanna's tears, her loneliness, and her waiting. That fear circumscribed my entire environment. It encompassed my walls and my cell. It enclosed my bed, my hour of sunshine, and even my prayers.

When Nanna stopped crying, she had much to say about love. Nanna spun eloquent words about love whenever she was in a good mood, she was in touch with her feelings, and her questions were absent. When she came to our nook, she lit up all the dark corners in the cells she passed by, even if their doors were locked against the sun. When she reached our nook, she carried me off to a time and place where the sun never set and the rain never blocked the sky—but only if she was in a positive mood. When she sat on her chair, her eyes stared into mine, glittering so much they made me dizzy—but only if she was in touch with her feelings. When she wanted to antagonize the cello player, she arrived in a dress that left no doubt as to who was the first lady in our nook and in our universe—but only if her questions were absent. When she sat on her bed and wrote, she loved me. She flirted and provoked, both gently and roughly. I embraced the letters so tight I nearly suffocated them. I went to sleep, covered in Nanna's scent, with her chest as my pillow.

Other times, Nanna kept quiet. Nanna was incapable of love when she surrendered, and her Eastern temperament was fierce in its victimhood. When she reached our nook, she would close the door quickly behind her as if pursued by ghosts during the long, dark trip here. She did not notice the faces of souls hanging in the cells on either side. Her fear was louder than their screams, her ghosts were larger. She avoided my eyes to hide her confusion. She looked around our nook and only saw its walls, not the suns that illumined it, nor the moisture-giving rains. When she spoke, she had much to say about her long days, her work, and the pain of her current case. I interrupted her with some talk about love. She hesitated, hovering at the edge of tears. When I stopped, she went back to what she had been saying before I interrupted.

6 November 2015

My soul:

How happy I am! The letters that reached me, and the visit that came afterward, have turned me into a ball of energy. When I lay my head upon your chest, Nasser, I think I will write the story of my return to my stolen village. Everything about you is impossible. Who else but you can make a woman feel the contours of her womb simply by mentioning the children he will give her? Do dreams really come true?

7 November 2015

We heard today about the passing of Djamila Bouhired, a great fighter whose sacrifices for her country helped set Algeria free.* That reminds me that I was too much of a coward to ask you about the torture you suffered, fearing I couldn't bear the details...In my work, we deal with many cases of torture against prisoners, and the details are always very painful. This Occupation has no religion. But you, Nasser, you are my religion. Yet how real are the pains!

8 January 2016

I told you that my year began very badly. But no longer! I received the photograph you sent me. Thank you, my dear, for creating this moment for me. Every picture of you is a work of art, and I know you did this to make me happy. Well, you succeeded! All my friends said how handsome you are—and I told them to back off because you're taken.

Nanna

*False reports of Bouhired's death circulated in November 2015.

"Nasser, that operation you told me about…"

"What about it?"

"It's not really necessary, is it?"

"It's not heart surgery. It will help me breathe more easily."

"But you could do without it? Without the operation, I mean."

"I think so."

"Then there's really no need to go through with it."

"Why?"

"You said just now that you don't need it."

"Nanna, what's the matter?"

"I'm scared. What's wrong with that?"

"I'll be fine! There's nothing to worry about."

"But they might…"

"No, they won't. I'm not the first person who's had an operation."

"Promise me you'll be okay."

"Okay, I'll promise, but only if you tie back your hair to show your entire face."

"Such blackmail!"

"You can always say no."

"Oh! I love you more than life itself!"

"Drive safe."

As if I hadn't suffered enough, it wasn't until my breathing got worse that the prison administration decided to perform the operation that would open my air passages. They scheduled a date, and it arrived. I was transferred to a nearby hospital under heavy guard. I didn't have long to wait, and within a few hours, I was in the operating room. When I awoke that evening, my mind raced through questions of who I was, and how and where I was. That lasted for many hours. Eventually the sedative wore off enough for me to become conscious of what was happening. I was chained to my bed, bound hand and foot. It was very late, so I surrendered to the sedative and slept. I woke a second time, still under the influence of drugs that muddled my thoughts...I hovered between waking and sleeping until a voice penetrated my lethargy.

"You're not allowed here."

"I'm a lawyer."

"Doesn't matter."

"I just want to reassure myself about him."

"He's fine."

"Let me go in to see him, just for a moment."

"It's forbidden. Don't you understand?"

"Then let me speak to him from here."

"That's forbidden too. You must go now; don't make me..."

I pulled back the curtain that shielded me from the voices. Nanna was surrounded by a forest of military uniforms and rifles. She towered above them all, and her voice drowned out theirs. Coming there was risky in the extreme. How easy for them to ruin her career! Yet she came. In her presence, the odors of death and gunpowder that filled that corner of the hospital evaporated.

Nanna was only a heartbeat away. Right in front of me, with no glass partition keeping us apart. She looked prettier and more beautiful than ever, despite how tense she clearly was. For the first time, Nanna believed in the truth of me. She was seeing me without any screens or barriers. She smelled my scent from nearby. If she stretched out her hand, she could have touched my body and my soul. Everything about her seemed trusting and believing. Lying before her, in a defined, tangible place, was the world she had been spinning: here was his wound, here was his bleeding, and here were the threads of blood. Everything seemed real in Nanna's eyes, even me, wounded and bleeding on my bed. It was me, wearing the chains she had never seen before. It was me, surrounded by guards and rifles. It was me, half naked, with clotted blood filling my chest.

How did I look to Nanna's eyes? Uninjured, unbound by any chains. Without any soldiers or guns in sight. She saw me in all my elegance and dignity, and it was her soul that filled my chest. That was the first time Nanna saw me and believed what she was seeing. No one could spin a world like Nanna. The very moment I was at the mercy of my sedatives, uncertain whether the scene was real or imaginary, was the moment she chose to see me for the first time.

I was afraid for Nanna on account of the soldiers. I struggled against my bed, and the handcuffs bit into my hands and feet. I struggled some more, but it was no use. My strength was no match for my bonds and the sedative, and I quickly gave up. How miserable are these bodies!

"Nanna, I'm fine. Don't worry."

"How are you feeling?"

"It was a simple operation, and there were no complications. I'm fine now, but you have to go."

"Okay, I'm going."

"Please tell everyone I'm all right, especially my mother."

"I will."

I had to sleep for many hours before I awoke and believed everything that had taken place. The intervening hours did nothing to spoil the wonder of that surprise.

21 January 2016

To Nanna's beloved:

My God! I still cannot believe that moment when you pulled back the curtain. It was my moment of triumph. Such a little thing, yet so amazing. Despite the fatigue, you were calm. You were so beautiful. And you were real. I keep replaying that moment in my mind, with you on your bed and no glass wall between us. I praise God that all this took place. Anything more, and I would have fainted from too much love...You are the only one who is able to make me feel this way.

Whenever I remember your face and the way you looked at me during those few moments we had, I feel a sense of assurance. That's what's behind the enormous wave of energy I feel. You are the one who has done this. You're the reason. Stop denying it! You are all my reasons, Nasser.

I wish I were able to stroke your head, to watch you sleep, to hold your hand, to kiss your forehead. But I apologize, O my heart's beloved, that I didn't do more, and that I wasn't the first person you saw when you woke up. Thank you for being my partner in that victory when our voices rose above theirs, and thank you for making me discover how far I'd go for you in my madness...I want you tonight more than anything. I'm praying for your recovery, without any setbacks.

Before our first kiss, would it be possible to try a sample? I confess, I'm just trying to steal an extra kiss. If only you knew how much I love you!

Nanna

Nanna showed clear signs of feeling sure about me. I could see that in our rare meetings in the visitation nook, and I could read it in her letters, though they, too, came infrequently during those months. But Nanna's variable moods soon came back, and so did her old fear, which began draining away her strength. Her fear was stronger now, and more violent. Without anything on the horizon to suggest my release and the union that Nanna had so long been anticipating, she sought out some farther horizon to distract her, if only for a little, from her waiting and from me. She bought a ticket to somewhere sufficiently far away, many thousands of kilometers, and left her fear behind—or at least, that's what she thought she was doing.

No distance is sufficient to save us from a fear that has taken root in our hearts. It buys a ticket for wherever we go. It sticks in our luggage and in our clothes, even if we've hidden it out of sight. It arrives before us and scouts out the places we've planned to visit, leaving behind unmistakable signs to remind us of its existence. Either before or after love appears, fear might enter our hearts, but it will never leave on its own.

It either takes its object and its causes when it departs, or else it remains for good. I was the object and the cause of Nanna's fear. She had to flee to the other side of the planet in search of pleasures that would muffle her screams and ease her pains.

Nanna traveled, and I was left with my questions and my fear for her. What am I doing here? What have I done to Nanna? The questions surrounded me on every side. The walls began displaying them in large letters. My fear grew until it was larger than me, and I assailed myself with accusations that always ended in condemnation. Nanna came to me, and I fell in love with her. But there I was, killing her slowly and deliberately, and writing letters and poems about her murder. She came to me, spinning her future out of my threads, while I remained immersed in my past and my present. She came to me at the end of her twenties, and I was in the middle of my forties. What am I doing here, and what have I done to Nanna?

Only rarely now did I soar off to be with her, for she no longer believed in these flights of mine. I hated that she spun a future only for my earthly body, which was incapable of joining her and providing the consolation she needed. Fear for Nanna followed me like my own shadow. It was with me in my cell, and it remained with me during my hour of sunshine. It left me when I slept, but it returned as soon as I woke. I fought against it every way I knew how. I attacked it, fled from it, confronted it, denied it, cursed it, and pleaded with it, yet still it brooded over my day.

In my ignorance of its vocabulary, I was frightened by this strange new fear within me. Nanna could have rescued me simply by walking out the door to save herself, but she locked all the doors, sat behind them, and cried. I tried surrendering to my fear. I wanted it to destroy me, but then it was pleased to keep me alive. It led me to the very edge of my anxieties and then gripped my wrist to keep me from falling in. If only it would drop me! My strength declined over the course of the subsequent months, which rapidly consumed my body until it was no longer strong enough to carry me. I neglected it further, hoping it might simply evaporate and vanish. Yet my body did not die. Somehow it kept going.

Nanna returned from her trip, yet every part of her wished she were still traveling. How can I heal from an injury that missed me and struck Nanna? How can I heal Nanna when I am her wound? I was tired of the questions. I was even more tired of my inability to come up with any answers. If only it were my wound, I would take myself off somewhere, either to heal or to die.

23 April 2016

Greetings, O my life!

Our recent visit was wonderful. Something close to magic! How can a small nook in a cramped prison turn into a dream? And how do you think there could be any substitute for this? If only I were as good at embracing you as you are with me. I know I often fail to reach the degree of connection that you expect of me, but how I love when it happens. If only it happened more!

I'm not someone who can betray herself just to fit into some framework or relationship that others will accept, so stop trying to tempt me with the idea of pulling back.

I know my waiting will contain difficult nights,
and I know I have to wake up from this dream. I tried
talking to my friends, but they aren't any help. I went
to my room to be alone, and I cried a lot... You are the
only person who can heal my solitude and my exile.
When will you come, Nasser? I need you so badly.
Everything about you is magical and attractive, and
everything in me yearns for you...

By the way, my last trip was so amazing that I've
begun planning another one soon.

Nanna

I prayed many times to my Lord for deliverance. I could no
longer bear the weight of the fear that had defeated me. I
could no longer bear Nanna's accusing tears. Nothing in my
fear or my pain resembled the dreams that Nanna wrote in
her letters. My pains were as real as Nanna was, and I needed
to heal from injuries that had not befallen me. Nanna was all
I ever wanted. Nanna was the cure for all my wounds, even as
I was her eternal wound that would never be healed. I prayed
to my Lord, calling upon all His names for help. I prayed for
so long.

I prayed to my wall, which I had abandoned, and which
had taken its revenge by becoming transparent. I called upon
all its names. I prayed for it to stop spinning me around,
together with the world around me. I prayed for it to restore
some kind of stability for me to grasp. Once again, I offered
my wall my old allegiance in case it would accept it and be

satisfied. I wooed it with my old flirtations. If only it would remember! If only my words would intercede for me! My wall remained silent, transparent, and invisible for many long months. From nearby, it observed my dizzy twirling and my burning. But I did not quit praying to it and offering my loyalty. I knew my wall's conditions well, but I wanted it to return without preconditions.

"Where are you?"

Silence.

"Won't you let me see you again, just for a moment?"

There was no reply.

"What more do you want?"

Still no reply.

"I offered you every sacrifice I possessed! Can't you forgive? Won't you be satisfied?"

Silence.

"If you're going to kill me, then do it, or else stop punishing me."

Silence.

"Say something! Say whatever you want!"

Silence.

"Does Nanna's presence here bother you?"

Silence.

"If either of us sees you, it's Nanna. She's the one who held fast to you when I let you go. Just ask her tears. Ask the curses she directs at your rigidity."

Silence.

"I'm tired. You're the only one who can save me from you."

Silence.

"Why won't you say something? Why won't you show yourself?"

Silence.

"Fuck you! And fuck me too, whether I hold fast or let you go."

Silence.

"Fuck my drawings on your ceiling! You've consumed my flesh: may it turn to poison in your mouth!"

Silence.

"Fuck my trinity: my bonds, the years, and the life sentence... Fuck the here and now. Everyone who comes here is already dead."

Silence.

I went on, but my wall maintained its silence. I spoke until I was exhausted. Then I fled to Nanna. I became calm as I settled upon her breast. I said a short prayer... and I fell asleep.

During those heavy months, I would escape my fear by sleeping. Those hours were the only peaceful moments I spent with Nanna, far from my fear for her, far from her crying. One day, I woke early, as usual. I kept my eyes closed, trying to postpone the encounter with my fear. But it couldn't last forever. I got out of bed to start my day.

"Nasser."

I was shocked to recognize the voice, but I did not hesitate for a moment.

"I'm here, O my wall!"

Love...and Yet

The things you choose to live for:
those are the things to die for.

—SOCRATES

I had accepted my separation from the wall, which meant the loss of my single point of stability. I longed for my end to come quickly and release me from the pain of a wound that afflicted neither my body nor my soul but was my wound nonetheless. The wound was in Nanna. Nevertheless, I bled before she did, and it cut deeper in me than in her. What did it matter if it was fear for Nanna that caused my death? Wasn't she all my reasons, including my reason for living? But death did not come to bring me peace and rescue Nanna from the grip of my imprisonment and my life sentence...Instead, my wall returned.

"I was afraid you weren't coming back."

"I never abandon those who hold fast, Nasser."

"But I didn't. I let go."

"And I waited for you to come back."

"I swear, I never cried for anyone like I cried for you."

"I saw. I heard you."

"I still love her."

"I hear it. I see it. I read it too."

"Does her presence bother you?"

"I like her smell and her taste in fashion."

"I'd almost say you were in love."

"Shame on you, Nasser! But haven't you seen her face?"

My wall returned without any preconditions regarding Nanna. It reconciled itself to her presence in our writings, our drawings, our scribbles. With the wall's return, my bright mornings came back, the hours filled with sunshine. No longer was I tormented by fear, ghosts, and anxious thoughts. Questions still hung upon my wall, but without their former intensity. The wall resumed its concealing opacity. Now the only thing I could see was Nanna, sitting on my bed and waiting for our bitter morning coffee. Our crying no longer paralyzed me. I no longer feared talk of love, which took up less and less space in Nanna's letters. I resumed my old soaring. I returned to Nanna in her hours of loneliness, exhaustion, and illness. I no longer cared if Nanna believed in my presence or denied it. I resumed loving her in the way I knew how. I forgave my body its impotence and its physicality. I forgave Nanna her spinning for my earthbound body alone. Once again, my hands forged their bonds of iron. Once again, my life sentence was a choice.

25 June 2016

Dear Nasser,

Our visit was unforgettable, just like the ones before it. You made me so happy when you described your plan to take all those trips with me, and you said it all without using any conditional phrases. Don't ever leave me, Nasser! Just thinking about it terrifies

me ... Soon we will be together, I know we will. I don't
know if it's possible to convey my feelings through this
page, but what I do know is that I've started to learn
what it means to make your face my home ... Do you
have any idea how wrapped up in you I've become?
Please, get out of prison quickly! I wonder what my
family's joy will be like when they meet you and get to
know you as I have. But the question remains: How
and when? Do you have specific ideas about how the
scene will take place?

Love,
Nanna

Nanna and I kept meeting in our nook. The meetings gradually became further apart, and only rarely did Nanna embrace
a sheet of paper to write about love or anything else. But nothing changed in the manner of my love or my writing. She
came to our meetings to catch her breath and to steal a couple
hours or more, during which she believed the world she spun.
Despite that belief, she cried, and I carried her to a place that
knew no tears. She spoke often about her strength, about
the legitimacy of her weakness, and about human nature. I
formed a safe zone that would accept and understand her if
her powers failed her and she surrendered.

But when Nanna left me and my nook, she found her fear
waiting for her behind the door. She believed that too, and
she renounced the things she had spun with me. I returned
to my bed with Nanna on my chest, certain of the integrity

and sole ownership of the spaces she occupied. But she returned to her car and closed the door. Sitting there alone, Nanna found no chest to receive her head, no hand to wipe her tearstained face.

Nanna's October approached. Arranging a birthday gift for her was even more difficult than usual, given everything going on at the time. Finding a gift that suited Nanna seemed like a mission impossible, but I did it. I devised a complicated plot in which my family and other relatives took part, and even other souls in the prison. I hid everything from Nanna to avoid spoiling the surprise. My gift reached her, and in some photographs that reached me, I saw tension and confusion on her face as she opened it. Yet when we next met, Nanna said she loved the gift, and that she loved me even more.

"It looks beautiful on your wrist."

"It does! It's exactly what I would have chosen for myself."

"It also chose you."

"Thank you, my dear! It really wasn't necessary."

"I didn't do it because it was necessary, Nanna."

"I know, but I don't want anything. You are enough for me."

"The search for anything to ease your mind has become my prayer and devotions."

"How did you do this? From inside prison, I mean."

"This bracelet felt lucky."

"You don't want to say. I understand. In any case, I'm the lucky one."

"How so?"

"It occupies my wrist, while I occupy your heart."

* * *

When we were together in our nook, Nanna made her peace with my confined horizons, but she cursed them when she exited into spaces that were broader and larger—or so people made her believe in a world of social conditions and expectations that defined Nanna's role, legitimatized certain frameworks, and forbade others.

What remains of love when we shackle it with various social and biological constraints? Can it possibly achieve fulfillment under this crushing avalanche of conditions? Why do we allow love to be translated into social frameworks and vocabularies, devoid of any real connection? How is love the condition that guarantees the survival of our species and our development into higher beings? How is love the thing that stops or slows our biological clock, that incessant voice that pumps the blood through our veins? When did we roll love out like a carpet, something that exists only on this earthly plane without ever looking up?

Nanna wrote things she no longer believed. In our nook, she spoke about love, but as soon as she left, the words evaporated and were choked by their own humid dust. She sat behind the steering wheel of her car, wrestling with the social and biological equations of her existence. Finding no solutions, she cried more and rarely felt secure.

Meanwhile, I returned to my wall, which embraced me and embraced Nanna in her fear. I returned to the conscious "I" that is reconciled to his environment in all its diversity. I returned to the Heideggerian person—an existence that creates its own essence. I resumed calling things by the names I chose, and I believed the miracle of my naming. Once more I loved Nanna, in our nook and any other space I made my own.

Nanna went on a second trip. She traveled to some other shore of the Mediterranean and to an ancient Greek mountain, crowded with gods that continue to spin their marvelous worlds despite their antiquity. She traveled, dressed in the sea, and baffled the shore and the seagoers with her colors. Unconsciously and on purpose, she flirted with the waves. She played with the black stones scattered across the beach. Then she returned to our nook. The threads of light on her body recalled an ancient Greek epic.

Nanna was away from our nook for nearly a full month. November had arrived, and so had Nanna's gift for me. But Nanna's letters stopped arriving. Nanna had stopped writing.

"Nasser, I want to tell you something."

"Why all this seriousness?"

"I want you to hear it from me before the next visit from your family."

"Nanna, what's wrong? You're making me nervous."

"The gift you gave me—I returned it to your family."

"You mean the one I just gave you, for your birthday?"

"Yes."

"Why did you give it back?"

"Because I don't deserve it."

"Enough with these riddles, Nanna. What's happened?"

"You looked everywhere for the perfect gift for me, even though you're here in your prison. And I had just decided to leave our relationship and pull away...Nasser, say something…I was weak and alone, and I wanted to run away from everything and from everybody and from you."

"So why didn't you run away?"

"It was just a moment, and it passed. I'm here now."

"It wasn't just a moment, Nanna. You made a decision."

"Yes, but I wasn't able to go through with it, so I came back to you."

"You came back because of your distress, or out of pity and compassion?"

"Stop it! I still love you. That's something I can never run away from."

Love does not grant us dominion over anyone. It does not legitimize our egotisms or the possessive tendencies within us. Love does the precise opposite. Love refines behaviors that we inherited in the moment humans left their forest caves. Love is creation. It is life. It is unending possibilities for surprise. Love is a divine spinning and the act of humans who become philosophers and semi-prophets. Love is the transient, temporal "I" catching a glimpse of the eternal "I." That's the tale I spun for my wall and proclaimed to myself before I met Nanna, before Nanna ever learned the arts of spinning and weaving the threads. That was the divine law of my vast cramped existence when Nanna came to search out her possibilities on the seashore across from the wall.

This was the Nanna I loved, desired, and felt passion for. This was the Nanna I chose to live with. And now she was in the deepest throes of her fear. She sat in front of me, showing nothing but fear and confusion. She sat there, a soul

dragging a body along the cliff's edge, numbed and stagger-
ing from exhaustion. No creation, no life, no surprise, no
eternity...Nothing in her resembled Nanna. Her eyes, which
used to light up our nook, held no glimmer. Instead of angels,
fear and ghosts swam in her face. Nanna looked at me, but she
did not see me. The music stopped. The cellist left our nook
without a parting farewell to either of us. After a few days,
Nanna went back to my family and reclaimed my gift to her.

My wall knew what I had to do. It approached and put its
arm around me as though suggesting something I had already
conceded.

"Nasser."

"I know."

"But I haven't said anything."

"You've said everything."

"I'm here if you need me."

"I'm not afraid, not yet."

"You'll always find me here."

"And if I let you go?"

"You wouldn't!"

"I did it once."

We let go so we can hold fast. There is no other way.
We hold fast on to love, but we let its object go so that love
becomes a choice—without conditions, without calcula-
tions, without an object. There's no dependence, no posses-
siveness, no jealousy, and no extinction. Love becomes an
object in and for itself. From nearby, I saw how love can be
choked by conditions and demands. Love enters a cage of
suspicions if any conditions are slow to be met, or if it unin-
tentionally fails a test.

Dismayed, I saw how love can transform into a monster that threatens the safety and balance of the lover. It twists the words of your passionate speech. It outstrips your steps and beats you to the heart of the beloved. It makes your chest a field of pains, devoid of water, grass, refuge. I feared the time when the feelings would change into equations beyond my ability to solve.

We let go in order to hold fast. That's what lovers do, either by choice or by necessity. My fear for Nanna overwhelmed me. Her fear overpowered her too, together with the conditions and equations she believed. I failed to inspire her with faith in my ability to soar through the air, up where the physical realm meets what lies beyond. Nanna hated the dry land, but when she came to plunge into our nook, she did not venture far from shore.

Do gods enter a confined space? Yes, but they don't stay long. When Nanna entered my small nook, she saw something that resembled the life she had spun for herself, an answer to all the questions she once posed to the sea. She sat there, exploring her possibilities and mine. She would leave for a time, only to return to her white chair to explore some more. She spun her conditions, and she sat and waited. She waited for one year. She cried for the second year. In the third, she sowed a fear that was about to destroy us both. My wall liberated me from my fear when it decided to come back and pull me close once again. Once again I loved Nanna . . . so I let her go.

Narrow, Crowded, and Old

December 2016. Our meeting was coming to an end. Nanna was talking a lot, sometimes about love, but mostly about other things, when without warning she suddenly burst into tears.

"What's wrong, Nanna? Why are you crying?"

"I'm afraid, Nasser."

"Afraid of what?"

"Of everything. Of all the pressures around me and upon me, of blocked horizons, of your life sentence, of your age."

"Of all that?"

"I'm facing it all alone, and everything is collapsing around me. You are here, and I want..."

"What is it you want, Nanna?"

"I want to be a mother."

"If our nook is keeping motherhood from you, Nanna, I'll kill it."

"Nasser, I love you."

"I know."

"But I'm tired. And afraid."

"I know that too, Nanna."

"It won't be long before our next visit."

"I'll wait for you."

I could no longer bear the suffering that I was causing Nanna. My love had taken her to the utmost limit of her endurance, but now all was spent. That was not at all what I had intended when I stopped denying my feelings for her. I had wanted to love her, to invite her on a long journey beyond the borders of this world. I was sure Nanna wanted that too, for the discourse she brought to our nook resembled the language of the sky people. I was surprised by her ability to read me despite the peculiar vocabulary of my unusual situation. I loved her in a way not permitted to mere mortals. I loved her beyond my abilities. I carried her across boundaries forbidden even to a man like me, who soars across every border. I loved her like someone born for that purpose alone.

How had my intentions filled Nanna's chest with painful wounds? How could I possibly go on holding fast to her if that meant her destruction? To keep loving her, I had no choice but to let her go. I wished she had kept her promise not to let my love transform into a monster that threatened her safety, and to tell me one hour before that happened. Then we would have stopped, and Nanna's face, lighting up the far reaches of the sky, would have been the last thing I saw.

Nanna departed our small nook, dragging along her disappointments at the impossibility of the future she had spun. She no longer believed her conversation with the sea one March day when she stood alone by the shore. Her sea had been agitated at that time, and she preferred to address it from a safe distance. But the road I took to my cell was safe and easily traversed. I found my wall alone this time, without Nanna pushing in to welcome me back. My wall looked nervous and tense. Its tension quickly passed.

"You've come back alone."

"Were you hoping for something else?"

"Where's Nanna?"

"She's left."

"Isn't she coming back?"

"She said this place was narrow and crowded and old."

"Did she really say that?"

"She did."

"But there's no one here besides me and your former Lord. So who was she calling old?"

"I don't think she was talking about you, so you can take it easy."

"Are you okay?"

"Nanna is okay."

"I was asking about you."

"And I answered about me."

"Are we okay then?"

"We will be. In a while."

I quickly made myself some coffee. It was the first coffee I had drunk alone since first laying eyes on Nanna. Its bitterness had a different flavor. Bitter like a parting. Then I began writing to Nanna about my lonely bitter coffee.

> Dear Nanna,
> Every time the world closed in upon you, and your fear of its bitter medicine increased, I used to flee from your fear to you. I would hold you close until your fear calmed down or went away. Not this

time. For my presence has become a burden upon
you, and I'm the last person you need when the fear
takes hold of you...

Nasser

A few days passed before Mazyouna came to visit, together
with my sisters.

"Are you sure?" asked my sister Inshirah.

"Yes."

"But she loves you! I hear it in her voice when she talks
about you."

"I love her more. Don't you hear that in my voice?"

"Don't you want to think it over?"

"I have."

"So what now?"

"I want you all to stay close to her."

"We'll do it."

"And to love her."

"We do, Nasser."

How do you set about letting go of the one you love? What
words do you begin with? Do you do it quickly, or do you
draw it out? Do you bring your confinement, your Lord, and
your wall, or do you spare her that trinity that has troubled
her for so long? Do you open with some final words about
love, or would that only give you second thoughts? Do you
come right out and say it, so you'll seem like someone who
finds it easy to part? Can your soul bear the fresh wound

that would come from looking at her face and her mouth, or her chest, where you no longer reside? What will save you if she cries one last time? Will you sit on your chair like you always used to do, or will you pretend it isn't there—for if you die, you want to die standing! Do you really care about any wound that kills you now?

It was 15 January 2017. I was sure of my path to the nook. And I was sure of my confinement, my Lord, and my wall. I was certain of my old faith and my story. I was reconciled with the things around me and their names. I was confident of my soaring, my wonder, my arrival. I had no doubt about the steps before me, which I knew were the last I would ever take toward Nanna.

We went together: me, my Lord, and a most confining place. I had let go of enough. We walked slowly, none of us looking at the others. It was as though each of us was preparing his final goodbyes on the way. The soldier escorting me opened the door. The wall went in first. Then my Lord. And finally me. I sat on my white chair, the wall remained standing, while my Lord surveyed both the wall and my tension. Then Nanna entered.

I was the only one Nanna greeted. She sat on the white chair, just like the first time, confused and tense, as though she were the one confined within those walls. My Lord kept watching, and my wall kept on standing there, both of them waiting to see how I would begin. I welcomed Nanna like I always did, asking how she was. But it was as though this person only resembled Nanna. Something about Nanna's presence foretold her absence, filling my aging, cramped nook with it. My Lord looked at me. I looked at my wall. There was no help there. While I was searching for some appropriate opening, Nanna knew exactly what she had come to say.

"Nasser, I've come to say something."

"I'm listening, Nanna."

"I've decided to break things off."

Just like that, without any preliminaries or any companions in a time of need, Nanna said what she had come to tell me. Quickly, sharply, decisively. Nanna hated to wait. That was the way she had spun her life from the very beginning, the beginning she chose when she came to announce she missed me. And when she lost hope in us, she came and spun us an ending in her own way too.

"I've told you before: here is a man who will love you no matter what, without any conditions or demands."

"I'm tired. I can't take it anymore."

"You've made the right decision, Nanna."

"I still love you, but I'm no longer strong enough."

"Thank you, Nanna. Thank you for every time my heart skipped a beat, for every breath that raced past, and for a life that was too short, even though what it contained was enough for me."

"Will you be okay?"

"There's no life after you, Nanna. I knew that from the beginning, and I accepted it."

I wanted to shorten that moment as much as possible. Perhaps as a kindness to myself or to Nanna, or else because I was afraid of emotions beyond my power to control. I asked Nanna to leave my nook, for the tears were starting to overpower her. She refused and went on sitting there. "Get out, Nanna!" I shouted. Nanna was still on her chair. I roused myself one last time and shouted even louder in her face, but there was still more she wanted to explain. I turned my screams to the guard outside the door. "Get me out of here!" No one heard. I began pounding on the door with a hand that wasn't mine. Nanna was afraid for my hand and quickly intervened.

"Okay, I'm leaving." She picked up her few papers and made her way toward the door.

"Nanna."

"Yes."

"Drive safe."

Nanna was gone. In the nook remained me, my Lord, and a most vast space. We returned to my cell in silence. My wall resumed its place, I was on my wall, and before my Lord left to manage His own affairs, He said:

"We didn't think you'd make it out alive."

"You didn't?"

"No."

"Were you scared for me?"

"How could we not be?"

"But why do you even care what happens to me?"

"Would you believe us if we said?"

"I can add it as one more lie to the pile of all mine."

"Now we know you've escaped!"

"But you haven't answered my question."

And then just like that, without hesitation or long preliminaries, quickly and in a sharp, decisive voice, they spoke together: "Because we like your company."

The Self

One obtains his existence through birth,
but he obtains his essence through his choices.

—ALI SHARIATI

I was born twice, and I was killed the same number of times. In the beginning, I was born from the womb of a confining camp that hung me for a short time upon its walls. It told a story I believed, and upon that story I built my many lies. I lived in the camp's center and upon the margins of an imitation city. I maintained my lies, my hanging, and my marginality until I was killed by a farsighted crusher machine, so blinded by all its killing that it no longer discerned what fell between its jaws. Then it hid the traces of its crime by burying me deep within a vault. Like someone who had been through it all before, I endured my killing and I lived upon the wall that was my grave.

I was born a second time from the womb of a concrete and glass nook. There, Nanna wove my threads and my accustomed lies until the nook was filled with old gods, swimming angels, and a cellist in red who played exquisitely. Nanna kept approaching, coming closer and closer until she believed what she spun. I believed it even more.

I was born from the womb of Mazyouna the first time, and the second from the womb of Nanna. Injustice killed the first baby; Nanna's fear killed the second. My nook wasn't enough for her. It was vast, but she only saw its narrow confinement.

"You are not enough for me. You and your faiths, your walls, your lies, and your fables about soaring. You are not enough for me. You and your confining nook, your vast universe, and your strange words. You are not enough for me. You and your wounds, and your partial wounds, and your promises of more wounds to come. You are not enough for me. You and your years, now growing so much older than my twenties."

Nanna didn't say any of that, yet she said it all. I was not enough. I lacked the conditions that would fulfill Nanna's emotional project. In me, Nanna saw a deficient man who would reach completion if the necessary conditions were fulfilled. Nanna saw what came after me, but she did not see me. From everything that followed our first meeting, Nanna spun a long poem, which she transcribed in her letters. She read her poem to me, sitting behind that stupid piece of glass. And when the flaws in what she had spun broke down, she scrapped the poem's publication.

In prison, I choose whatever space pleases me. I conclude a long, complicated discussion with the Creator of the universe regarding His creation and His existence. I make my bed in the clouds, high above anything that might shield me from the moon's company or a shooting star that has decided to make a swift, final plunge. I organize my earthbound hours and my evenings with friends so that they do not interfere with the assignations that women schedule with me. I choose the place, the time, and the colors of the clothes they wear. I never repeat the same words of love, nor do I kiss the same mouth twice as I sow my grass across their bodies.

In prison, I am master of this wall, of every wall before it, and of any wall that might come after. I am master of these balconies and all they look upon. No one enters my garden or plucks the breast of my women. I am all my evenings and every nightfall. I am the morning's thirst for the late-arriving sun; I am the day that clings to me. I possess the sun's hour and the hour's sun, and every hour of the day. I am lord of this nook, lord of the cell, lord of my life sentence, lord of this ceiling, the lord of waiting. This is my vault.

"You are not enough for me," said Nanna.

In my prison, I am the master of my things, the one who bestows their names. If I wish, I change them, and if I wish, they stay the same. I am my prison, and I am the prisoner. I am the witness of my lost cause, and I am the martyr. I am bereaved of my freedom, and I am my freedom. I have a beloved in every Nanna. I am the lover, and I am the beloved.

"You are not enough for me," said Nanna.

In prison, I am the abounding destitute, the addicted believer, the swift-moving slow, the happy mournful, the laughing crier, the vast confinement, the floundering swimmer, the losing winner, the renegade devotee, the dissolute ascetic, the haughty toiler, the excellent sower.

"You are not enough for me," said Nanna.

In prison, I am Nasser, Mahmoud, Samih, Hamza, Muhammad, Ahmad, Malik, Abd, Muhannad, Faris, Mansour, Walid, Khaled, Sa'id, Ammar, Ammad, Alaa, Adil, Asim.

"You are not enough for me," said Nanna.

In prison, my wall is me, and I am my wall. These are my things, and those are their names.

"You are not enough for me," said Nanna.

This is my cell, this is my tomb, here are my words. I swear, I've never had a living home more precious to me than this dwelling of mine.

"You are not enough for me," said Nanna.

This is me, this is my Lord, this is my vast confinement.

"You are not enough for me," said Nanna.

This is my cry. Nothing more than a single phrase that does not rest and is never choked off, a cry that continues forever: Nanna, give me back myself!

Finished on 6 July 2019 at 1:18
Hadarim Prison, cell 33

Translator's Afterword

Luke Leafgren

The responsibility placed upon a translator is always a weighty one. I have never felt that burden more than with this project.

In every instance, a translator undertakes the audacious task of representing an author in a new language. When seventy thousand words in one language, meticulously chosen and arranged with care, are replaced by ninety thousand words in a very different language, opportunities abound to fail, in small ways and large. Even if I had a perfect command of language and style in both Arabic and English, the charge would be daunting. In this case, the author for whom I am speaking is in prison. He cannot express himself freely in any language. He has fewer opportunities to reach his audience, and a limited scope to correct or clarify anything I get wrong in my translation. So the words I choose for the book bearing his name count more than ever.

Moreover, I have never attempted a translation that felt so urgent. One reason I translate is to help authors connect with an audience. Nasser Abu Srour has been in prison for more than thirty years, and any delay in translating his literary memoir would stall someone who has already waited so long to share his creative voice with the world. A second reason I translate is to open doors of understanding for those who wish to follow me through, and the message of this book could not be more pressing. It clearly articulates the Palestinian's experience of alienation within their own land, and the loss of dignity and hope that has resulted from the Israeli occupation. Even before the appalling killing in Israel, Gaza, and the West Bank that began on October 7, the urgent questions of the Palestinian people were unanswered for decades and worsening.

Little did I guess the full significance of an email I received at the end of June 2022 from Other Press, asking if I would like to translate a sample for a book they wanted to publish. It arrived while I was crewing on a sailboat delivery from Cherbourg to Helsinki, and the unrushed tempo of the trip allowed me time to start falling for this book. I felt an immediate connection with the narrator's existential questions about life. I was intrigued by the ambitious collage of genres and styles—autobiography alternating with historical, political, and psychological analysis, moving vignettes of adolescence and of prison life, a love story told with poetry, dialogues, and letters, all framed by the narrator's relationship with the personified wall of his prison. I saw an opportunity to use my energy and abilities to promote the Palestinian cause of dignity and self-determination.

Within a few weeks, I submitted my translation of three early chapters. After a conversation with Other Press publisher Judith Gurewich, I signed a contract and began work in earnest in September. Four months later, in mid-January 2023, I finished a first draft of ninety-seven thousand words. After an intensive round of editing with Judith—over email and in reading sessions at her home, a ten-minute bicycle ride from mine—the second draft of eighty thousand words was finished by the end of March. Other Press was moving fast, but they allowed me time to set the manuscript aside and approach it with fresh eyes during the summer. In late July, I spent an exquisite week editing the final draft in Hurghada while waiting on repairs to the dismasted sailboat I was motoring from Jeddah to Cyprus. (One last round came later, in November, when the managing editor generously permitted me an additional 450 tweaks, my favorite kind of edit, to the typeset proofs.)

The responsibility I felt for this project was all the greater because I had assumed the role of editor, working closely with Judith to shorten my initial draft by almost eighteen thousand words. We believed we could reach a wider audience by compressing the text to accelerate the pace of reading. That meant leaving out a number of examples, abbreviating or deleting certain sentences, and removing some paragraphs we felt were less essential. To make the text as engaging and readable as possible, the syntax and punctuation became somewhat more direct in places than I found them in the Arabic manuscript. I occasionally added definitions or cultural context to the text to help the reader understand things the original audience would know. Throughout the process, we were committed to preserving the range and complexity of Nasser's ideas and to expressing them accurately, while also maintaining Nasser's characteristic way of layering reflections upon each other.

It is uncommon for a translator edit a text to this degree, and the task did not come easy for someone who grew up with a reverence for authors' words and a belief in the sacrality of texts, both religious and literary. Moreover, the stakes were high: Nasser's story matters, both to him and to the world, and I was terrified of getting it wrong. Yet the reasons to bring Nasser's book to a broad audience justified the attempt. This book is an important work of literature, telling a unique story in a unique way. It brings attention to Nasser's imprisonment, pressing the question of whether his trial and sentence were just.

While authors of books in English often work with publishers in this way and benefit from the perspective of editors before a book goes to press, such collaborations are less common in the Arabic-language publishing world. In any case, that would not have been possible for this text, given the author's limited ability to communicate with the outside world. It seems a miracle that Nasser was able to find some way to convey any manuscript at all to his prestigious Arabic publisher, Dar Al Adab.

I was reassured by feedback from Nasser's friends and relatives who read portions of the translation and commented that my words echoed in English the way they heard Nasser's voice in Arabic. We were even able to get a draft of the edited translation to Nasser in prison. He sent back corrections throughout the manuscript and endorsed my decision to omit one of the poems. In addition, I feel deep gratitude for all who have provided advice or comments on my work throughout this past year: from among Nasser's family and friends (including Shatha Abu Srour, Jamal Abou Srour, Nadia

Daqqa, and Nidal Al-Azza), Judith's team at Other Press (including Yvonne Cárdenas, Lauren Shekari, Gage Desser, and John Rambow), and other friends (including Kareem James Abu-Zeid, Yousif Hanna, and Amara Yakhous).

Translation is a weighty responsibility, and it comes with the knowledge that perfection is as impossible as the task is vital. But it is also an incredible privilege to take part in the creation of literature, and to stretch my abilities with a text as intricate and varied as *The Tale of a Wall*. I hope, of course, that readers will appreciate this translation; even more, I hope they will be inspired to read the Arabic source, translate Nasser's poetry, and discuss the meaning of Nasser's works until such time as he is free to join in the conversation.

Cambridge, Massachusetts
December 2023

NASSER ABU SROUR was arrested in 1993, accused of killing an Israeli intelligence officer, and sentenced to life in prison. While incarcerated, Abu Srour completed the final semester of a bachelor's degree in English from Bethlehem University, and obtained a master's degree in political science from Al-Quds University. *The Tale of a Wall* is his first book to appear in English.

LUKE LEAFGREN is an Assistant Dean of Harvard College. He has translated seven novels from Arabic and has twice received the Saif Ghobash Banipal Prize for Arabic Literary Translation, in 2023 for Najwa Barakat's *Mister N*, which was also short-listed for the EBRD Literature Prize, and in 2018 for Muhsin Al-Ramli's *The President's Gardens*.